Awakening the Essential Feminine: Claiming Your Influential Power

Maureen Simon

Printed in the United States of America
First Printing, 2011

Printed in compliance and in good standing with
Sustainable Forestry Initiative® (SFI®), Programme
for the Endorsement of Forest Certification™ (PEFC™),
Forest Stewardship Council™ or (FSC®).

Library of Congress Control Number 2010940803

ISBN 978-0-615-41300-6

Essential Feminine Publishing
P.O. Box 613
Mill Valley, CA 94941
www.TheEssentialFeminine.com

Graphic Design & Layout: Zoey Setiawan, *www.ZoeyChloe.com*
Final Design & Layout: Kip Williams/Print-Ink Press
mrkipw@gmail.com
Digital Art: Victor Lee *vlee317@gmail.com*
Cover Design: Leslie Waltzer, *www.crowfootdesign.com*
Editor: Nanette McGuinness *nmc22@cornell.edu*
Book Photographer: Sam Hassas
www.hassasphotography.com

Dedication

To Brigid, the suffragettes,
my mother Mary, my father Tom,
my dear husband Karim,
the many sisters who have enlivened my life,
and God's nature and many gifts.

*In every being there exists a masculine and
a feminine nature. The masculine side reveals
itself as the powers of discrimination, self-control,
and exacting judgment qualities that express
or respond to reason.
The feminine nature consists of feeling—love,
sympathy, kindness, mercy, joy.
In the ideal being, these two aspects are perfectly
balanced. But if reason lacks feeling, it becomes
calculating, harsh, judgmental; and if feeling lacks
reason it becomes blind emotion.*

Paramahansa Yogananda

Author's Note

In order for our world to be fair and harmonious, we need to equalize those areas where equalization has not existed in the past. We must strengthen women's voices and deepen our understanding of our gifts and talents for this equalization to occur. This book offers an opportunity for women to understand and claim some of the innate talents, gifts, and abilities that the feminine holds. I believe that women are predisposed to these feminine gifts by the very nature of our birth, biology, and socialization. We are now poised in a perfect position to bring the pendulum back to center, where the masculine and feminine can live side by side, empowering each other and fully utilizing the gifts of both.

Women hold up half the sky.

Chinese proverb

*When sleeping women wake,
mountains move.*

Chinese proverb

Acknowledgments

Linda Alvarez
Danielle Amar
Cherie Arnold
Karim Belaid
Bellevue Club
Xavier Durand-Hollis
Debra Evans
Judie Fouchaux
Bonnie Gallup
Sam Hassas
Victor Lee
Gina Liberman
Lorraine Lyman
Camille Maurine
Nanette McGuinness
Khadija O' Connell
R. Zoey Setiawan
Nancy Shanteau
Martha Sperry
Leslie Waltzer
Martha Weiner
Kip Williams

Linda Alepin and the fine women of the
Global Women's Leadership Network, Santa Clara
University, California

The Metropolitan Club of San Francisco

Special thanks to: Bonnie Gallup, a dear sister and colleague who worked together with me closely for over a year gathering the research that has made this book a reality; Karim Belaid, my loving husband, who has given me wonderful support as I developed The Essential Feminine™ Company for the past twelve years; and Judie Fouchaux, who has stood by me, through all our highs and lows, as we both knew that we had a purpose that was stronger and greater than the both of us. I also hold much gratitude for Nancy Shanteau and her amazing skill talent and over all support, and to Zoey Setiawan for her beautiful design skills, fine eye and for making this book beautiful.

Table of Contents

Introduction

I was first inspired to write this book when it became clear to me that women around the world were unaware of their natural feminine talents and power and of the influence that these assets hold when fully expressed. I realized that our lives can be far more satisfying, successful and meaningful when our feminine nature is fully contributing to all areas of our lives. I noticed that women were climbing the ladder in business and knocking off the women who were coming up behind them in order to win in a highly competitive narcissistic world. Through my individual consulting with business women worldwide, I noticed that women were experiencing a decreasing level of satisfaction in business and life. I began to wonder what was contributing to the feelings of dissatisfaction and disharmony.

About fifteen years ago, I began to study feminine attributes. I looked closely at women's natural gifts and tendencies. I saw that a majority of women are comfortable in building relationships, collaborating, and caring for others in the world. I noticed that we communicate with great agility and have the ability to engage others collaboratively in both dialogues and projects. I observed that when women speak, we express emotions comfortably and are often able to communicate with ease. I saw many, many more abilities in addition to these and began to make a study by watching friends, observing clients, and reading books. Three years ago, I began to do anecdotal and subjective research on this topic with my friend and colleague Bonnie Gallup. We did extensive research on feminine attributes in business and in life. I have used this research to inform my comments and observations in this book.

Through my research, I realized that the feminine qualities of care, compassion, the ability to create and sustain deep relationships, the values of peace and harmony along with the many other feminine talents and attributes were not valued and prioritized in the world where powerful decisions are being made. Their absence is reflected in the facts that women hold less than 8% of the board seats in major international corporations and earn $.80 on each U.S. dollar in comparison to their male counterparts.

We can also see the absence of feminine attributes reflected in the number of violent wars currently on this planet. As a mediator in the disruptive wars in Northern Ireland and Eastern Europe, I had firsthand experience that war destroys the lives of children, families and communities for generations beyond the end of the conflict. As the one who births life it is a woman's natural feminine instinct to provide the care, safety and security her family needs. She needs to be at the table where these decisions are made.

Masculine and feminine attributes live side by side in men and women. Women are predisposed to our feminine gifts due to our basic biology (brain and hormonal, etc) and because of the way we are socialized. The Essential Feminine qualities place us at a distinct advantage in today's world. When we become aware of our unique attributes and gifts, and of the critical value and potential influence that they hold in today's world, our world will become a much more positive place to live. Women contributing the feminine perspective will bring more diversity and harmony to the decision making tables.

In recent years, women have fought dedicatedly to achieve a status that places us as equals (in our minds, at least) to men. We have proudly climbed the ladder, particularly in business, and have pulled up our trousers, learning the ways of thinking, working and succeeding in a masculine world. I strongly believe that the masculine aspects of our nature are very much needed in life, but if they are over-weighted, the world will continue to be off balance with excessive wars, misuse of power and abuse of the environment. I have written this book to support women to learn, claim, live and lead with their Essential Feminine. I believe the feminine is now needed in order for us to reach equilibrium across all areas of life. The time for the feminine to meet and compliment the masculine has come. The outcome of this union will be to save this amazing world we all inhabit.

Awakening the Essential Feminine: Claiming Your Influential Power focuses on the nine areas of life in which our feminine attributes, gifts, and talents are predominantly and uniquely expressed. These areas include: relationships; harmony and peacemaking; thinking; imagination and vision; creativity and innovation; language; power; intuition; and beauty and aesthetics. Within these 9 areas of life the book identifies twenty-six attributes, gifts, and natural styles that women hold and that serve as magical keys to creating a shift from an isolating, masculine, power-based, autocratic world to a web-like, compassionate universe.

I hope that you will enjoy this book and that it will provide you with an opportunity to dream big, step outside of your comfort zone, and contribute in the best way you can. Enjoy the journey you are about to embark upon. Today's world needs you to step forward more than ever before.

Maureen Simon

Philosophy

I have a strong respect and reverence for men and their masculine gifts. Some of my greatest teachers and guides have been men—including my father. While the attributes that I describe in this book are shared between both men and women, I am drawing attention to the ways in which their brains, biology, values, and socialization make women unique. Men may cultivate the feminine qualities of an attribute, just as women may cultivate the masculine qualities of an attribute. That is the beauty of the masculine and feminine living side by side. However, this book is intended to support women as they identify, claim, and live with their feminine qualities as strengths that will allow them to increase their contributions to the world as leaders, decision makers, and creators of new and innovative ways to live.

When women understand their importance in the world today and really understand that it is time for them to claim a greater capacity for growth and change, they will begin to lead with greater confidence than ever before.

I believe that we must:

- First, fully understand the attributes, gifts, and talents that are unique to the feminine. Once they are fully understood, we must make them our own and become comfortable with these gifts and talents.

- Next, we need to look around the world and see how our natural gifts can make a difference.

- And finally, we must lead from a place that brings us out of ourselves and allows us to make a contribution to the whole, whether as a mother in her home or a powerful leader in the external world.

In this book, I am not claiming that all comments and observations are based on pure, empirical, scientific research. Rather, my interpretation is based on subjective and anecdotal information and experiences. The bibliography serves as a road map for you to gain access to additional, more empirical background information.

The book has also been heavily informed by my individual and group work internationally with thousands of women over the past 25 years. These women and their life experiences have enriched my knowledge of the feminine and have provided a deep understanding of the attributes I discuss in this book. The clarity and knowledge that I have received about the Essential Feminine has been the focal point of most of my professional life; I have created an entire "body of work" around the Essential Feminine in order to empower women to create success and influence in business and in life through my webinars, classes, CDs, and consulting.

The philosophy behind *Awakening the Essential Feminine: Claiming Your Influential Power* has also been informed by the work of Rutgers University anthropologist Helen Fisher, author of *The First Sex: The Natural Talents of Women and How They Are Changing the World.* Other key sources for our research include Louann Brizendine's *The Female Brain* and Carol Gilligan's *In a Different Voice,* as well as Helen Palmer's *Inner Knowing.*

How to Use This Book

Awakening the Essential Feminine: Claiming Your Influential Power has been designed to take you on a journey through the natural talents, gifts, and attributes of the feminine. While you may choose to read the book from cover to cover, it is not mandatory. You may decide to focus on any individual area as you read the book, or, if you want, you can put it down, pick it back up, open it with intention and intuition, and read the section you open to, as it may relate to a question or concern in your life.

This book stands alone as a guide to support you in learning about your Essential Feminine gifts and talents. It can be used as a part of your meditation and self-reflection process, or it can be used in a gathering or a circle. As you read through the book, you will see that each chapter covers a specific area of the feminine and begins with an opening invocation, opening ideas for contemplation, an introduction to that area, inspiring questions, and the invitation to be witnessed if you want to create movement or change in that area.

Additional material to help you on your journey can be found online at *www.TheEssentialFeminine.com*, where you will find further information to support you on the way. Future companion tools in the works include a journal and a deck of Awakening Your Essential Feminine cards.

Read the opening invocation as you begin to sit quietly, either together in a group or circle or on your own. This is a time for you to invite the guidance of the Essential Feminine.

Opening Ideas for Contemplation

This poem or quote has been provided as a source of inspiration as it relates to the attribute you will be examining or discussing. It—or they, as there may be more than one—is also intended to provide a moment of reflection and an opportunity for inner connection.

Inspiring Questions

I have designed three questions for each attribute. These questions can serve as an impetus for deepening your personal connection to the topics covered as part of that attribute. When answering these questions, notice your first response and then continue to listen deeply for ideas and thoughts that follow. Look for further information that may come through after your reflection on the question. It is in the deepening of your inquiry that you will receive meaningful guidance. As you reenter the world and continue to live your life, look for divinations, coincidences, and synchronicities that may support the information that you have received or that further your learning.

Witnessing

After you have answered the inspiring questions referred to above, decide if there is an action, commitment, or intention that you would like to make as you move forward in your life. Be sure to speak your intention, as there is great power in stating an intention and being witnessed.

Women's Groups and Women's Circles

Each chapter of this book examines one of the nine areas in which the feminine is uniquely expressed. These areas can be explored individually as you read the book on your own, and they can also be brought into a women's group or circle where the exploration of the Essential Feminine and its attributes occurs in a rich community dialogue.

If you are gathering in a women's circle, you can bring a specific area to the group for dialogue and discussion, or you can use each of the nine chapter areas as content for facilitation. Simply read through the material in each section, allowing time for conversation and reflection. Sessions can be set up to discuss each of the nine chapters or chapters can be consolidated. As the group comes to an end, consider witnessing an intention set by each woman in order to take advantage of a new revelation or learning brought forth from working with *Awakening the Essential Feminine: Claiming Your Influential Power.*

Part I:
Enlivening the World
through Feminine Expression

Chapter 1
Relationships

Relationships

Opening Invocation

The feminine holds great richness in her ability to build and nurture relationships. Her deep understanding and valuing of relationships form the web of life. In her life she prioritizes sharing, including, connecting, and communicating. Her care, compassion, and empathy keep the flame of life alive.

Opening Idea for Contemplation

> *...One does not choose between 'the rational, goal-oriented, and just' of the masculine energy and 'the irrational, cyclic, relating' of the feminine energy; instead the idea is to hold the tension between the two.*
> *—Helen Fisher*

Introduction to Relationships

Being overly autonomous, independent, competitive, and action-oriented creates an environment of isolation, power mongering, and self-centeredness. The competitive, overly-individualized culture in the United States developed from a militaristic model that encourages hierarchy, competitiveness, and aggression. While this model has served the growth of America well in past years, it has become outmoded and obsolete in today's world. There are many

examples worldwide of societies that encourage support and care for the needs of all. We now must move to a model that includes compassion and concern for others in a non-competitive, inclusive, relational way.

Our current, self-centered, less relational orientation can be harmful, as it does not always serve the good of all. Today's model focuses on benefiting the few who hold power and make decisions. For years it has been felt that if you share information, you dilute your power, and if you place a high priority on communication, you lose control over situations and people.

Since the feminine values the whole over the parts, is interested in direct communication and collaboration, and often enjoys sharing power as a means to building relationships and sharing knowledge, her gifts and talents are needed in the world now in an unprecedented way. Because the female is the more relational of the two sexes, we move away from disharmony towards peace and choose to build relationships that provide nurturing and care.

In this book, the chapter on relationships launches the first of nine areas where the feminine most predominantly lives, and includes the importance of collaboration, inclusiveness, interconnectedness, communication, care, compassion, and empathy. Time and time again in our research, we have found that these various areas can be traced back to the feminine and her role in the family, community, and society.

By first identifying your personal relationship with each of these areas and then evaluating which of these areas would enrich your life if enlivened, you can develop connections to the world that open many new doors and horizons. Through relationships, we learn most of all about ourselves and the world that we live in. As you develop a deeper understanding of how connections with others influence your life, you will have a greater ability than you now have to use your feminine gifts and talents to explore, develop, and grow rich, meaningful, and wise relationships.

Inspiring Questions

1. Where in your life could you collaborate with or include another that would benefit both of you?

2. How can you connect more to others, outside of yourself? What would be the benefit to you and to others?

3. Where can your communication more deeply reflect how you feel?

Witnessing

Make a commitment to enrich the relationships in your life. State the commitment aloud after completing the reading on relationships and their attributes.

If possible, be witnessed by a friend or someone who supports you.

Maureen Simon

Collaboration

About collaboration

Women understand that no one woman can hold all knowledge. Women have a distinct understanding that when we listen to others, include their thoughts, and get them to be a part of an agreed-upon direction before we take action, we will have better results. This approach leads to inclusivity. The greatest benefit that collaboration offers is the understanding that everyone is a leader, as opposed to one person. Collaboration also encourages direct communication. When communication is direct and flows freely, we open the door for understanding. This builds flexible and diverse dialogues, work environments, and political exchanges.

Why collaboration is special to the feminine

From the days that women washed clothes together on the shore of a river, they came to know the importance of working together. This included watching each other's children and taking care of community tasks. Women have an innate sense that when we are aware of the needs of others, we benefit the whole. At times, collaboration has been seen as a by-product of indecision, but in reality its consultative nature brings about the best decisions, thinking, and actions.

How women can use our gift of collaboration

People need to be a part of something and to be valued for what they can offer. When we collaborate, everyone feels a sense of ownership, and this sense of ownership leads to greater success and a deeper level of involvement from everyone than would otherwise be possible. It has been shown repeatedly that women maintain networks based on relationships that allow them to connect diverse environments. This ability allows women to contribute our full resourcefulness, together with our natural gift of collaboration. Our ability to relate to many diverse people and styles allows women to build connections across many groups throughout life. Many believe that this desire and urge to connect has a strong link to estrogen and begins in women at puberty.

Why collaboration is needed in the world now

The world has become a very individualistic place. Many people only look out for their own interests and disconnect themselves from what would benefit the whole, the world, or the whole of others' needs. It is time to keep the benefits and creativity that individualism allows us while we focus on what will better serve all. We gain people's buy-in and support when they feel their input is included. There has never been a greater time in the history of the world than now, when people need to feel part of the larger whole and in collaboration with others. We have created much separateness through social class and inequality. We must now build bridges that allow our world to become far more egalitarian than it currently is.

Remember collaboration when...

...you feel insecure and become competitive or feel like focusing on winning at all costs to achieve a goal. Remember collaboration when you feel the need to make a decision and are unclear or unsure of which direction to go. Think collaboratively when you seek deeper levels of creativity and support than you might achieve on your own.

Enlivening collaboration in your life

Surround yourself with people who are aligned with your way of thinking, but do not exclude from your circle those who will stretch or expand you. Look around your world and notice the people that you want to bring onto your team. Create a salon or a gathering that supports you and others on topics that encourage your growth and creativity. Play or make music, dance, and move with others.

Inclusiveness

About inclusiveness

By nature, women innately include others in sharing decisions, information, and power. We value others' opinions and involvement, as we understand that this collective involvement leads to strong decisions and outcomes. When we include others authentically, with pure intention, we build deeper relationships. We enhance a web that we know to be the essence of our connection with others. When this web is strong and expansive, it moves us away from hierarchy and allows a more equal, holistic relationship to unfold.

Why inclusiveness is special to the feminine

Because of our understanding that all are important and all voices are needed, women are drawn to the voices of other women, for those voices have been excluded in the past. It is also natural for women to be inclusive and to involve the voices of many. In addition, women are also less prone than men to holding to a single authority. Since women have a natural desire to connect, share power, and include others, they are well positioned to integrate silent parties and to support others in the full expression and contribution of their voices.

Women see themselves in "the middle of things" (web). We do not see ourselves at the top (hierarchy). We build flexible, diverse, and cooperative work environments. We are trusting and have an impulse to share information that holds a concern for relationships and connection. We are naturally interested in sharing power.

How women can use our gift of inclusiveness

The feminine has been minimized in our world. It is now time for women—who are strongly predisposed to the feminine—to step forth and show the power and contribution that the attributes and gifts of the feminine hold. Inclusiveness is one of the main strengths of the feminine. We must not be afraid to lead and to show our gifts and talents in the world.

Leadership takes many forms. Becoming a leader and part of the collective with a voice that is valued brings personal responsibility. It is easy to look towards the top, to the one who leads us, but it is far more rewarding to look within and to the circle around us, to the powerful team that we are a part of. When we share power, we naturally include others. This builds more flexible, diverse, and cooperative environments than hierarchical power structures. We are the leaders that we have been waiting for. All voices must now be heard.

Why inclusiveness is needed in the world now

The world needs for each of us to be our own leader now. In the past, one person held power and knowledge. It is important today that knowledge and power be distributed, in order to create the critical thinking in business, politics, and life that is essential to the continuation of a sustainable, equitable, and enlightened world. Old paradigms of leadership place power at the top. The leadership that the world now needs places leadership at the center where all converge, and encourages the inclusion of many voices.

Remember inclusiveness when...

...you notice an unbalanced sense of power permeating a project or activity or find yourself using power in a way that puts you into a superior position. Notice times when you have knowledge or something to share and find yourself pulling back or isolating yourself. Remember to include others in your life when you have something to teach or share. When you feel an innate sense to build relationships or when you seek to make a contribution or build your knowledge base beyond your individual capacity, it becomes essential to include others. Remember to look to your elders, ancestors, and history to include wisdom that may be far beyond you and your years. In our role as the caretakers of children, we need to listen to and include the wisdom and needs of our youth. Their wisdom allows us to bring the world into an increased balance through their ability to see life simply and clearly. We must now include the wisdom of our children and our elderly in our days and our lives.

Enlivening inclusiveness in your life

Reach out to include diverse thoughts. Build relationships in places and with people that are new to you. Look for diversity and ways to build bridges in your everyday life. Include someone in an activity or event that you would normally not think to include. Begin to see things in new ways through the eyes of others and allow yourself to walk in another's shoes in order to open your heart fully to our unique differences and diversity.

Interconnectedness

About interconnectedness

We are all interconnected in many ways. Some ways are obvious to us and others are invisible. When we live with the understanding that we exist in a whole, complete system and that we, ourselves, only provide a small part of the whole, we then allow our awareness to reach out beyond ourselves and deeply connect with the lives of others. When we are concerned about how our or another individual's actions affect the whole, we begin to heighten our awareness of this naturally connected world in which we live. Women and the feminine have an innate sense for the connection that lives in and between all parts of the system of life.

Why interconnectedness is special to the feminine

Because the feminine is interested in how an action affects the whole, we naturally focus on the whole versus the parts. The feminine is highly relational and is interested in points of contact that connect people, allowing for deep exchanges, strong relationship-building, and communication. As natural peacemakers, we tend to have a strong interest in building bridges and looking for common bonds that allow us to strengthen our relationships and relate to others from areas of shared interest. The male brain often focuses on one segment or issue at a time. The female brain has a natural ability to connect diverse thoughts and concepts with greater ease than the male, due to the female brain's well-developed connective tissue that links the right and left hemispheres of the brain. (More on this in the chapter on the attribute of thinking.) This ability provides us with a tremendous asset in a world where fragmentation and separation have resulted from an extreme expression of individualism.

How women can use our gift of interconnectedness

Having the ability to look at the whole of a situation and the gift to understand the connection between the diverse parts of a whole, women are in a position to make major contributions. Women naturally have an overview perspective, which provides us with rich solutions, deep collaborations, and the ability to go beyond "just reaching the goal." When we stay connected to the interests of the whole individual, community, or world, we naturally include the needs of all as we work towards a single goal. This interconnectedness allows us to experience the rich joy and benefits that the journey towards a goal holds.

Why interconnectedness is needed in the world now

The tension in the world today between cultures, religions, territorial power, and socio-economic diversity

has caused many separations. At the end of the day, each of us is working toward creating the best life that we can. When we take apart the boundaries that the mind has invented and allow for interconnectedness between people, cultures, and societies, we begin to realize that we are all similar in many ways and that the differences we once perceived as threats are actually healthy diversities. When we begin to value deep connections, we experience respect and dignity based on equality, which includes reverence for our differences and commonalities.

Remember interconnectedness when...

...you focus on your individual needs or treat winning and being your individual best as lifetime priorities, for you then miss the whole story and a whole realm of possibilities. This often separates you from others, and you become blind to the gifts that your relationships with others hold. Notice times in your life when you feel self-centered or selfish. We often have a natural gauge that is built into our intuitive being and lets us know when we are being extreme in one way or another. Notice when your desire to achieve or win hinders, excludes, or demeans another.

Enlivening interconnectedness in your life

Travel to a country that you have never visited. Eat food that allows you to understand the geography, climate, and natural resources of a part of the world that you least relate to. Read the story of someone's life in a faraway land. Look at pictures of how others live in community. Notice where their abundance and scarcity lie. Make a gift or a contribution to someone who has great need and lives either near you or in a distant land. Walk in nature and notice how all species interrelate and interconnect to create a vital ecosystem.

Valuing Communication

About valuing communication

The feminine views conversation and communication as ways to cultivate connection and trust, not just as vehicles for expressing a message. When we share intimate personal information, we show our vulnerability and deepen our connection with others. What we choose to share reveals what we value and invites others to share their values with us, increasing our collective information and power to work together as a team.

Why valuing communication is special to the feminine

Because women are capable of communicating from our personal experiences and vulnerabilities, we share a part of our spirit that allows us to connect deeply with others. We cultivate closeness through our conversations and often show discomfort with communication that includes conflict and encourages separation. It has been shown that our talent for verbal expression is universal across cultures and that young girls are gifted with the ability to find appropriate words and create sentences faster than boys (Gilligan 58). To the feminine, conversation and communication lead to power, as we find strength in knowledge and connection.

How women can use our gift of valuing communication

Communication involves the act of speaking and being heard and the act of listening and acknowledging the words of another. Once we understand and claim the feminine's natural gifts and skills in the area of communication, we can begin to model authentic communication. Our strength and confidence in this area make it easier for others to do the same. The golden key to powerful and strong communication lies in our ability to listen actively and with care, for when we do so, we teach others the value of being heard and of listening. When we honor and value communication, we honor the people in our lives.

Why valuing communication is needed in the world now

In today's fast-paced world, people do not feel fully heard or valued. When our listening and conversations are relational and caring, people feel increasingly safe to contribute and to be involved. When people share intimately, on an equal basis, they more readily express their creativity than they might otherwise. When we communicate on an intimate level, we allow more of our true selves to enter into the conversation than in more neutral communication. And when we are comfortable sharing creativity, information, and power, we work and live from the highest possible levels of collaboration, expression, and contribution. This leads to a world of richness, innovation, and fully realized potential.

Remember to value communication when...

...there is something in the world that you feel strongly about and you believe that the clarity of your voice can make a difference. Remember times when you need to speak up for your own personal rights and beliefs. Notice times when you hesitate due to a lack of confidence. Discipline yourself to clarify and express your thoughts. Learn how to engage others' desire to listen to you without losing your personal style, story, and message. Believe that your opinions and observations matter and will make a major contribution. Notice when you hold back from speaking. Figure out why. Ask for help in clarifying your thoughts, strengthening the tone of your voice, or finding ways to present your message, thoughts, and ideals. In moments of conflict, step forward when an issue or cause requires your input. Notice what is right for you and find ways to communicate that are not threatening or destructive. Find ways to shed light and wisdom on a given situation.

Enlivening the value of communication in your life

Notice what you love about the way you currently communicate. Notice times when you have been successful in getting a message or idea across. Build on your strengths. Begin to observe times when you feel

shaky, unsure, or threatened in communicating with another. Take the situation apart and learn what it is that makes you feel weak or vulnerable in that moment. Get help from another in strengthening your voice and speaking clearly. The world needs your voice, vision, and clarity now more than ever before.

Care, Compassion, and Empathy

About care, compassion, and empathy

Care, compassion, and empathy comprise the threads that hold all life together. When we are cared for in a compassionate way, we feel a sense of peace and safety that allows us to move forward in the world with confidence and trust towards others. When we have truly been heard, respected, and supported through empathy and care in our life, we are likely to carry these values forward in our relationships with others. Once grounded in this sense of being seen and accepted for who we are, we can create anything.

Compassion includes the ability to have concern for another and to have the ability to share and connect to how another feels. This can manifest as a deep, unspoken level of understanding another. When we understand the joys and tribulations of another, we begin to empathize deeply. Care and compassion are essential values that we need to cultivate in the world today. When babies are held and touched, they develop at a faster rate than when they do not experience touching. Care, compassion, and empathy hold the seeds that support all life at the highest level.

Why care, compassion, and empathy are special to the feminine

The feminine holds the ability to bring forth life, which is the ultimate act of care. Through our ability to nurse and keep a being alive, we possess the ability to care for, respect, and value all life. By our very instincts, we know that care is what kindles growth. A woman who is aware of her innate feminine attributes and gifts knows that when care is given, the recipient blossoms. When living with her feminine gifts fully enlivened, a woman is naturally aware of all of the world's children's needs and is capable of watching over their safety simply from her instinct and nature. This care is natural to the feminine.

How women can use our gifts of care, compassion, and empathy

We now need to begin to understand the richness that care, compassion, and empathy offer the world. A crying baby is often handed to a woman to calm. We need to know that the calm we are naturally capable of instilling in a child is the very calm that we must instill in the world at those times when disharmony thrives. Just picture a world where you, yourself, showed care on a daily basis in the lives that you touched and where you extended compassion to someone who needed your help—a world in which your ability to relate empathetically was the norm. What a wonderful world this would be!

Why care, compassion, and empathy are needed in the world now

People in the world today need to feel heard, understood, and valued even more than ever before, as interactions in today's world so often lack these qualities. Many people in the world today have not had these influences in their lives. Therefore, the world reflects this void. If we create business, political, and community environments that are formed from the concerns of all and that meet human needs through care, compassion, and empathy, we will create a different exchange and vibration in the world—one that leads us to understanding, respect, and peace.

Remember care, compassion, and empathy when...

...you meet someone who is uncared for, alone, or in need of your ear or voice. Start the day by noticing where you could more fully express care, compassion, or empathy. Notice where there is a void of these gifts and observe the effect that this void has on a person or situation. Begin to live with and model these gifts so that others can begin to do the same.

Enlivening care, compassion, and empathy in your life

When you, yourself, need care, compassion, or empathy, seek it. Learn to meet your own needs in these areas, as you will then be able to support others at

a much higher level than if you do not do so. Create a daily practice where you rotate through a day for care, a day for compassion, and a day for empathy, and start to notice how these attributes could become more alive for you throughout your daily interactions. Discover an area where you feel a strong affinity or commitment and find a way to volunteer or make a contribution in this area. Notice your interactions in the workplace and with family and friends. Where could you express these attributes more strongly? Remember that when you are conscious about your interactions and take action to elevate them, you create a ripple effect of benefits that travel across all people, places, and time. Pay your care, compassion, and empathy forward to serve others and the world. It will no doubt act as a boomerang and come back your way.

Chapter 2
Harmony and Peacemaking

Maureen Simon

Harmony and Peacemaking

Opening Invocation

The feminine prefers to avoid conflict, since it compromises our ability to stay connected. We enjoy collaboration and joint participation in decision making. We tend to formulate requests as proposals rather than orders so as to avoid provoking confrontation. The world now needs, more than ever before, the economic stability, safety, and harmony that comes with the feminine's natural contribution to harmony and peacemaking. We have a personal responsibility in the area of harmony and peacemaking as the level of unrest and disharmony that we personally carry in our soul and our being directly relates to our ability to bring peace into the world.

Opening Ideas for Contemplation

> *Happiness is when what you think, what you say and what you do are in harmony.*
> — *Mahatma Gandhi*

> *If ever the world sees a time when women shall come together purely and simply for the benefit of mankind, it will be a power such as the world has never known.*
> — *Matthew Arnold*

Introduction to Harmony and Peacemaking

It is not necessary to have conflict in order to have power. In an environment of harmony and peace, our human potential increases greatly. People must feel respected, involved in decision making, and valued for their unique contribution in order to build cultures of harmony. Studies have shown that estrogen contributes to women's deep drive to connect with others, to achieve harmony and consensus, and to work and play in a more equal fashion (Fisher 41). Women understand that peace and harmony are not signs of weakness, but rather signs of strength. We have an innate desire to protect our own and other species. Growth and expansion are not possible in the face of violence.

Women naturally gain power through harmonious connections and use language to gain consensus and influence others. The use of language, as opposed to guns and ammunition, allows for time to negotiate and find amicable solutions to challenging problems and situations. Many women work to avoid conflict at all costs. Since women often try to settle disputes without direct confrontation, we have much to learn in order to bring our communication to an authentic place in situations where actual conflict arises. Our main challenges are to avoid suppressing our personal views and interests to accommodate others and to speak with strength and clarity about what we value.

The current state of the world is one of disharmony, and many parts of the world are presently experiencing violence and domination. These troubled areas are sites of destruction and pain, which are often the result of greed, a desire for power, and a lack of respect and interest in the needs of others. It is wrong at this time in the evolution of humankind to have people living in subhuman conditions–without even food–and in communities where land mines destroy life and limb and prevent the cultivation of the land. We now need to move to a higher level of consciousness than ever before to create a world where daily fear and danger in people's lives, homes, cultural values, and traditions are not tolerated—anywhere across the globe.

It is absolutely essential we each develop our own way to find peace and clarity in our lives. This peace and clarity directly effects how we relate to others in the world and how they relate to us. This cycle is ancient. If we individually find a way to create peace within ourselves, we will see greater peace in the world. For years I have practiced Transcendental Meditation™ (TM) and other powerful meditation techniques. TM is a good way to create peace within yourself and the world in which you live. I have also been inspired by the work of Paramahansa Yogananda and the wealth of knowledge that the ancient Celtic tradition offers. There are many paths to peace and conscious living.

Women are natural peacemakers, as we prioritize connections and work to reach agreement (Tannen

167). When we are in conflict, it threatens our ability to stay connected and build bridges of harmony, attributes that are, once again, part of our nature. For many women, war seems senseless, destructive, and purposeless because, as the bearers of children, we hold a concern for all. This is why it is essential that women move into more prominent positions of leadership than they currently inhabit, so that the feminine values that we naturally hold can be a part of the decisions that are being made in the world today.

Inspiring Questions

1. Where in your life could you use more harmony and peace?

2. How can you begin to create a life where harmony and peace are abundant?

3. Is there an organization that encourages peace and harmony that you would like to support? If so, how?

Witnessing

Notice the positive energy, creativity, and innovation that you experience daily when you increase the levels of peace and harmony in your life. Make a commitment to increase the peace and harmony in your relationships. If possible, be witnessed by a friend or someone who supports you.

Maureen Simon

Women's Approach to Harmony and Peacemaking

About harmony and peacemaking

The feminine possesses a natural desire and predisposition to create harmony and make peace. She prefers to avoid conflict, as it compromises her need to stay connected and to nurture. She uses language to gain consensus and influence others, often without telling them directly what to do. This allows the feminine to walk the line between getting what she wants and maintaining and developing meaningful relationships.

Why harmony and peacemaking are unique to the feminine

The female brain has greater control over the way anger is expressed than the male. The female brain structure is developed to exhibit 20 times less aggression than the male brain. Since the feminine prioritizes collaboration and the needs of the whole, she prefers to settle disputes without direct confrontation and tends to formulate requests rather than dictate orders. This moves her towards her desired results and lessens the possibility of confrontation. Many researchers believe that girls have been programmed to keep social harmony, and that starting in childhood, they live comfortably and happily in the realm of peaceful interpersonal connections. In play, girls tend

to participate jointly in decision making with minimal stress and conflict, as social connection is central to their being. Many studies indicate that estrogen contributes to women's deep drive to stay connected with others and to achieve harmony. Whether due to estrogen, socialization, or a combination of both, the feminine undoubtedly highly values and prioritizes peacemaking and harmony.

How women can use our gifts of harmony and peacemaking

When women learn to balance their true voices with their innate ability to seek harmony and peace, we will have mastered the ability to build greater levels of collaboration and cooperation than now exist. When we realize that men use conflict to establish status and that they are generally wired to avoid compromise, we can better understand how they experience and express themselves in the world. Once we realize that men use conflict to establish status, this helps us understand the current level of aggression in the world, as men are at the helm for the majority of the decisions made about most wars on the planet. When we begin to understand the source of excessive aggression and misused power, we have an opportunity to create inspired change. It is clearly time to evaluate how and why we are experiencing global and local conflicts and to illuminate these conflicts, excess competition, and senseless exchanges that occur. It is time to realize that the gifts of the feminine are now needed to create models and exchanges that include more joint participation in decision making and that eliminate conflict that stems from the misuse of status and power.

Why harmony and peacemaking are needed in the world now

The world holds enough unnecessary conflict today. Compromise and compassion lead to connection and peace. When we learn to think before we take action or react, we create a more thoughtful, meaningful response than otherwise. When we begin to consider issues without competition and status, we allow the space to explore fully, communicate, and develop the true outcome or best direction in which to proceed. When we encourage people to be involved and participate in discussions and decisions, we build increased agreement. Sometimes there can be a creative tension when we work to achieve what we want, for we value maintaining a given relationship. But those who have a developed sense of how to keep harmony and peace learn the skills to respect their own needs while they honor the needs of others.

Remember harmony and peacemaking when...

...you desire superficial power for your own personal benefit and/or omit the voices and desires of others. Still, remember not to suppress your personal power, views, and interests in your pursuit for peace and harmony. Consensus is important, but make

sure you take a risk and disagree, so that you stay true to yourself and live authentically. Learn to find a balance.

Enlivening harmony and peacemaking in your life

The world is now crying for harmony and understanding. We must first have peace within before we can bring true, deep peace and harmony into our daily lives and our world. There are stages of learning and connecting with inner peace. Include meditation, inner reflection, prayer, and/or contemplation in your daily life.

Begin to notice where in your life you currently lack harmony or peace. This can include relationships, environments, and even the peace that your mind holds. Eliminate these discordant aspects or make changes that will allow you to hold harmony and peace in your own life. Take one action in your life that will bring you closer to peace and harmony. Describe it in your journal or to a friend. Practice this action daily for one month.

Chapter 3
Thought

Thought

Opening Invocation

The feminine is gifted with a flexible mind that has a great capacity to encompass growth and welcome change. She can live in the moment, since she works for the good of the whole in the long run. The complexity of the world does not stop her from accomplishing and creating; she can do and see many things at one time, for she has the ability to see the whole and to build relationships between people, places, and things.

Opening Idea for Contemplation

The biological reality, however, is that there is no unisex brain. The fear of discrimination based on difference runs deep, and for many years, assumptions about sex differences went scientifically unexamined for fear that women wouldn't be able to claim equality with men. But pretending that women and men are the same, while doing a disservice to both men and women, ultimately hurts women. Perpetuating the myth of the male norm means ignoring women's real, biological differences in severity, susceptibility, and treatment of disease. It also ignores the different ways that they

*process thoughts, and therefore perceive
what is important.*
– Louann Brizendine, M.D.,
The Female Brain

Introduction to Thought

History is filled with satires, jokes, and comments about the differences between the ways that men and women think and perceive the world. Even more jokes exist about women's ability to multitask: to handle more than one thing at a time and simultaneously bring them all from start to finish. Men often perceive this gift as being scattered or fragmented and lacking focus. In truth, it is a fine art that comes from the structure of the female brain. In contrast to the male brain, which is accustomed to compartmentalizing problems and seeing things in black and white, the female brain has great flexibility and suppleness, enjoying a great capacity for change and growth.

Women also have a natural ability to take a broader perspective than men—to hold onto a world view or concern for the whole as a primary interest and focal point. When it comes to solving complex world issues, the masculine brain tends to want to solve the immediate problems at hand and to see immediate results. This penchant for shorter-term thinking can at times lead men to perceive feminine thinking as being stuck in a state of "analysis paralysis," unable to take swift, decisive action. To the female brain, the male's "firefighting" approach to problem solving, especially in business, often waylays longer-term strategic planning and relegates it to a low priority. To the female brain, the future matters. The feminine often questions what legacy we will leave our children, for she holds a long-term view.

When women begin to understand and claim the assets and unique gifts that come with the feminine brain—and often with female thinking—we will begin to use these gifts as strengths instead of liabilities. For many years, a linear, decisive, outcome-based way of thinking has been considered superior to a process-based, inclusive, flexible one, but the former has often omitted the needs of our local and global community, the environment, and our legacy for the future. It is now time for women to trust our unique way of seeing and thinking about the world. The challenge for us is to bring forth our unique style as an asset and to stand firm in the importance of our approach, viewpoint, and impact on decisions, ways of thinking, seeing, and, ultimately, treating each other with respect and dignity.

The opportunity before us offers the chance to bridge different styles of thinking, so that we can reach decisions and experience outcomes that will take the best from all viewpoints and be of service, both now and in the long term. In order for this to happen, we must understand and respect the differences between male and female thinking. The many laughs that have occurred throughout history because of the differences between men's and women's ways of thinking can be our richest resource moving forward. If we can look at these differences with humor and respect and go on to eliminate all mean-spirited judgments, communication between men and women will be elevated to an entirely new level.

Inspiring Questions

1. What issues, situations, or needs where you can make a difference are of most interest to you in your family, community, or the world?

2. Where does your gift of being able to do more than one thing at a time come in handy?

3. Where could you seek more input and advice when making an important decision?

Witnessing

Notice what you are thinking and feeling after having read about this attribute. Notice if this is an area where you feel you need to gain strength and understanding or to make a commitment going forward. If possible, be witnessed by a friend or someone who supports you. Check back after a week and see if anything has shifted, changed, or expanded.

Maureen Simon

Mental Flexibility

About mental flexibility

Because of the structure of our brains, women have a natural ability to consider a wide range of data and to perceive and understand relationships between people, places, and things. This biological advantage allows us to multitask, work with advanced concepts, and see all aspects of a situation. These gifts lead to a great capacity for growth and change. Psychologists have established that men think and plan according to abstract principles in a more focused, structured way than women do. In meetings, for example, men make more categorical statements of right and wrong, and they often see things in terms of black and white, whereas women speak from personal experiences and include numerous details.

Why mental flexibility is unique to the feminine

The study of anthropology has taught us that ancestral women began to develop mental flexibility as they cared for infants, fed crying children, and kept everyone warm and protected during severe and challenging times. As these outstanding skills and capacities developed over thousands of years, they influenced the architecture of the female brain.

Research has shown that this difference in architecture between male and female brains stems from genes on the X chromosome that produce women's mental flexibility as well as many other aspects of feminine mental acuity (Fisher 15). The cables of connective tissue that connect the two hemispheres of the brain are also different in women's and men's brains. One example of this increase in tissue thickness can be seen in the corpus callosum, one section of which is thicker in women than in men according to studies done by Lacoste-Utamsing and Halloway (Fisher 11). The second main tissue bridge that connects the brain hemispheres is the anterior commissure. This band of fibers is 12 percent larger in women than in men (Allen and Gorski, from Fisher 11). It is believed that this increased tissue thickness allows women a greater flow of comprehension and information between the right and left hemispheres, which supports mental flexibility.

How women can use our gift of mental flexibility

Today's complex, multifaceted, and fast-paced world requires us to multitask, act quickly, and think clearly. We must hold competing and disparate pieces of information and respond with complex and holistic solutions, rather than applying a black-and-white, rules-based model. It has also become important to have a full and complete understanding of a whole system or a whole being, as this deepened understanding elevates our ability to make thorough and informed decisions.

Why mental flexibility is needed in the world now

Having the ability to see and understand complex relationships between people, places, and things builds understanding. When we fully understand and integrate the needs of complex relationships into our perception of the whole, we create win-win solutions.

Flexible thinking encourages growth, innovation, and change. These are characteristics that women naturally possess, both in brain function and cultural socialization. The masculine brain has been shown to have less natural ability to adapt to changes and challenges than the feminine brain. Our world today requires that we develop new systems and ways of living on the planet: it is time for flexible, open, non-compartmentalized, creative thinking to prevail. The feminine can be a great teacher and leader in this area.

Remember mental flexibility when...

...you need to focus or produce more than one outcome in a short period of time. Realize that you most likely have a unique gift in this area. Look for the assets that your gift of multitasking offers. For thousands of years, your brain has been developing to handle multifaceted, complex situations. Take a step back,

evaluate the situation, and make decisions that will allow you to live clearly and productively. Remember that your brain has been formed to understand the relationships between people, places, and things, to consider and work with a wide range of data, and to be able to be flexible and open to growth and change.

Enlivening mental flexibility in your life

In order to create clarity of mind, which enhances mental flexibility, take time out to contemplate and regroup. Allow yourself to move away from the reins of your busy mind and find the quiet, spiritual place within. The mind's great flexibility is your gift, but the mind needs rest and rejuvenation. Close it down and let it relax. Then rejoin it when you have given it a break, meditated, and listened to your own internal, quiet voice.

Long-term Thinking

About long-term thinking

Long-term thinking is the ability to take a broad perspective, think contextually, and see the whole over time. The feminine has a strong tendency to plan for the long-term, for we keep the protection of our overall species in mind. Long-term thinking requires us to be aware of our immediate actions, so that they may provide a benefit over time. We also must consider the impact of our present actions on our own futures. This type of thinking is based on wisdom; it requires us to live with foresight and respect for life and our environment.

Why long-term thinking is unique to the feminine

We consider the long-term effect of decisions because we have a deep and sensitive connection to life. Being the bearers of life—the overseers of the little ones and the environment into which they will grow—we have a strong concern and connection to the conditions under which we and our children grow and thrive.

Because the female brain has a diffuse awareness that takes in more details and constructs a more complete picture of our current reality than the male brain does, we are more naturally adept at keeping our whole field of thought open and at living with

tension and paradox. These gifts for sorting information allow us to move openly and to incorporate the constant changes that we face in today's world into our thinking and actions (Frenier 20, 85).

How women can use our gift of long-term thinking

Women need to claim our ability to engage in long-term thinking and to see it first and foremost as an asset. We need to be aware of the fact that we are the ones who carry the burden of protecting the whole, so that we can act accordingly. This includes our ability to protect the environment, be involved in the creation of a peaceful world, and take a leadership role in major decisions that are being made in our world today. As women hold a deep understanding of how important the future is, those of us involved in politics and business are talking more and more than ever before about the legacy that we will leave our children. This foresight is critical to our world today.

Why long-term thinking is needed in the world now

As we reach crucial decisions about the ways that we live, and take inventory of the damage humans have inflicted in the areas of global warming, violence, and insensitivity to people and planet, we—as the child-bearers, with our innate gifts to see the whole—now hold a new level of responsibility to speak up, communicate what we see, and take action. The short-term thinking of simply gathering power, which leads from self-centered interests and lacks any concern for the depletion of resources, has gotten us into a position where long-term thinking is critical for us to move from survival to a state of thriving.

Remember long-term thinking when...

...you have thoughts and observations that you know you need to make known. Never be afraid to speak up. Start by asking questions to inspire others to think. Know that your observations and thoughts have value. Never prematurely silence your voice. Think critically and actively about the future impact of a current decision and about how your actions and thoughts can make a contribution to further the safety, growth, and evolution of the world in which you live.

Enlivening long-term thinking in your life

Identify issues that you need to be aware of now that may impact your and others' future lifestyles and quality of life. Make a decision about what you are ready and willing to do, be, or say, so that you remain honest and in line with what you value and believe. Have conversations that allow you to share your awareness and intuition. Notice which non-profit organizations and issues interest you, and commit to contributing time or money to them. Create conscious, open-ended intentions for your future and

your long-term contributions and interests. Picture the world as you would wish to see it. Creating this picture is the first step in realizing your dream.

Comfort with Ambiguity

About comfort with ambiguity

Women are comfortable with ambiguity and look to find solutions for challenging, ambiguity-filled problems. This is one of our natural gifts. In addition to seeing the broad perspective on both sides of an issue, we have the ability to hold the tension of opposing needs and concerns. We also are good at constructing relationships between unrelated ideas and concepts. Going back in history through anthropological studies, we find that ancestral women served as mediators and peacemakers. Our comfort with ambiguity has led women to incorporate uncertainty and change naturally into our worldview and into the way we live and make daily decisions. Women have a natural ability to work creatively with obstacles, challenges, and the unknown.

Why comfort with ambiguity is unique to the feminine

The feminine holds within her nature the ability to live with paradox, accepting that something is true even though it may clearly conflict with something else that may also be just as true. Particularly capable of seeing either side of an issue—as well as both—the feminine also has the ability to pull together intricate relationships from diverse ideas. Her ability to embrace ambiguity is helpful in creating solutions in business, as well as in creating strategies and planning for the long term. When unexpected changes arise, the natural ability to create alternate options becomes a great asset in a variety of environments. Seeing the broad picture, once again, provides for a deep understanding and concern for the whole.

How women can use our gift of comfort with ambiguity

There are times when a linear focus is needed to accomplish a given job, and there are times when having a broad perspective and seeing both sides of an issue—while holding the tension of opposing needs and concerns—are essential. The latter requires a relaxed, open form of thinking, one in which closure and immediate action may not be part of the process. When we keep the broad perspective in mind, we allow for a bigger picture to be taken into account than we might otherwise have done, and we often are able to take many viewpoints and needs into consideration. This encourages fairness and builds relationships, while solving problems.

Why comfort with ambiguity is needed in the world now

Because our world today holds much uncertainty and we sometimes experience discomfort in our daily lives, ambiguity—which the feminine is naturally comfortable with—freely inhabits our lives and our world. As we move into leadership positions and

model our gifts as mediators who reconcile many diverse ideas and as leaders in environments that need outcomes and solutions, we have an opportunity to use our strengths to create powerful and meaningful long-term solutions, instead of seeking immediate closure and short-term, band-aid fixes.

Remember your comfort with ambiguity when...

...you are forced to solve problems and get closure in situations that you do not yet feel you completely understand. Remember that black-and-white thinking limits your ability to see the big picture and take creative solutions and considerations into account. When asked to be linear in your speaking and thinking, realize that this may not be your natural style and may reduce the complexity of your understanding. Although showing confusion, a lack of clarity, or indecisiveness may place you in a vulnerable position, hold true to your process and realize that this comfort with ambiguity will often lead you to a meaningful, productive solution or outcome.

Enlivening comfort with ambiguity in your life

Notice your level of comfort with ambiguity. It is a feminine gift that results from our brain structure, but the level of comfort with ambiguity varies from person to person. Notice when you are being forced into a quick answer and respond in a way that is

natural to you. Give yourself permission to sit with the unknown. The world moves quickly; we need to slow it down. Take time for contemplation, reflection, and inner listening. Gather many opinions before you make a decision. Assess the inner and outer information that becomes available to you.

Community Focus

About community focus

Women realize that in community lies the life force and connection to the whole that is required for our overall existence. Therefore, we think in terms of "we." We naturally form inclusive communities and provide nurturance and support for others, all of which enable our communities to grow. The feminine values the security and connection provided by networks of relationships and considers the creation of family, neighborhoods, and villages to be of great importance. We recognize that it truly does take a village to enhance the development of the individual and ensure that our society honors and respects all.

Why community focus is unique to the feminine

Women tend to be interested in cooperation, harmony, and connectivity. We seek networks of support. We thrive in webs of relationships. We are naturally adept at making lateral contact with each other that manifests itself in cliques, circles, and supportive groups. Women know how to invite and offer support when and where it is needed. We hold a diffuse awareness that focuses and prioritizes relationships over things. This helps us to understand the strong feminine desire to create, affirm, and preserve life.

How women can use our gift of community focus

Women have a natural ability to build relational networks. As these networks merge, they have a compounding effect that expands the network and allows each member to access the resources of the greater whole. This results in expedited business development and facilitates the accommodation of needs and the sharing of solutions. When we realize our strengths and areas of interest and share them, we begin to move from isolation to connection. It is in our sharing in a community and in the relationships we develop that we have our greatest opportunities to learn, grow, teach, and make a difference.

Why community focus is needed in the world now

Much of the world is now aware of the reality and importance of our interconnectedness. We share the same planet and are interdependent: the air we breathe, the water we drink, and the food chain that we eat from affect all of us equally, for the earth sustains us all just as equally, no matter who we are or where we live. A mother in Nigeria has the same instinctive concern for her child—and for the earth—as a mother in the USA. Over time, we have learned that hierarchal, self-focused ways of being serve neither us nor the good of all. We are now much more aware of our mutual reliance than at any other time in history. By understanding the very basic importance of networks in our world, we can encourage relational models to become the norm in business, politics, and community life. Most people on the planet today are learning that greater power is realized when we share our concern for the planet and all life than when we remain isolated.

Remember your community focus when...

...you feel like you are losing yourself in your giving. Always remember to feed and take care of yourself first, because it is from your own strength that you will be able to be of service to others and support them. Women are natural givers in their community and family lives, but it is important for us also to learn how to receive. Be open to receiving, because your ability to receive is a measurement of your ability to give. When you limit what you are open to receiving, you limit the joy and the potential of the exchange. This is a natural law and directly affects your ability to be totally present and alive in a community.

Enlivening your community focus

Notice the communities that you feel included in. What are you giving? What are you receiving? What are the needs that you have in a given community that remain unmet? Where do your greatest challenges in relating to others lie? Are there other communities of interest that you have not approached or connected with? Where can you share your networks for the greatest benefit of all? Communities are a

source of joy and sharing, and of giving and receiving. When issues or challenges arise between you and others, notice any learning that is relevant. Express yourself fully and grow in the community.

Maureen Simon

Decision Making

About women's decision-making abilities

Feminine decisions are based on a holistic and comprehensive thought process. The feminine takes both detail and important criteria into account. We look for input, advice, and collaboration when we gather information. We search for a perfect decision that includes all of what we want, for we consider the needs of others instead of focusing solely on our own needs. Indeed, the feminine often puts others' needs before her own when making decisions. In this new age that we are embarking upon, it has become important for women to claim our voices in the decisions that are being made about our lives and our world. It remains important to seek advice and collaborate as we gather information, but it is equally important that we step forward and make sure our needs are expressed and cared for in the decisions we make and in our daily lives.

Why this style of decision making is unique to the feminine

As noted previously, the female brain includes cables of tissues that connect the two hemispheres of the brain, with one bridge, the corpus callosum, thicker in women than in men. This physical advantage affords women the opportunity to balance information and make decisions based on diverse information. The

feminine also lives centered in a web-based model, as opposed to a top-down, autocratic one and, therefore, she processes information, makes decisions, and gives advice from a clearer, more balanced and informed perspective than the masculine. Our diffuse awareness takes in everything and allows us to perceive clearly what is real and important in the moment.

How women can use our decision-making abilities

When we strongly claim our ability to make balanced, clear decisions and understand that this ability is based in physiology, we begin to gain confidence and hold an increased self-assuredness about the decisions that we make. When we claim and live from the place of understanding that our decisions are holistic, comprehensive, and detail-oriented and that they include important criteria, we will gain even more strength. As we continue to build confidence in the decisions that we make on a day-to-day basis, we will begin to contribute at a higher overall level than before in the world in which we live.

Why women's decision-making abilities are needed in the world now

We live in a complex world in which we cannot make decisions in an overly simplified manner. We need to include all the details in order to respect and include the needs of all. When we learn to value our own advice and our natural ability to collaborate, we will

begin to realize more buy-in and participation from others than before. It is an important time for us to believe in ourselves and the decisions we make.

Remember decision making when...

...you need confidence in a decision that you are making or you take your life to a whole new level and your confidence feels less than solid. Begin to trust the still, small voice within, the information that you are highly skilled in gathering, and your ability to include complex information in the decisions that you make. These factors elevate the level at which you make your decisions to a higher one than you may currently be using, as they more fully reflect holistic thinking than otherwise. Also remember your unique and highly developed ability to make decisions in moments when you are challenged and questioned. Include all the variables and take all the time that you need to make decisions that reflect your values.

Enlivening decision making in your life

Notice people in the world who are making decisions. Who do you respect? Who do you question? Observe the areas of your life in which decisions have been challenging for you to make. Find support and models of people that you can turn to for advice and to help build your confidence. Listen from an inner, intuitive place and notice the level at which you are able to make decisions that reflect your authentic voice and values. Notice if a decision feels good or bad, as this

feeling informs and directly relates to the level of consciousness and awareness with which you live your life.

Part II:
Igniting the Creative, Verbal, and Imaginative Side of the Feminine

Chapter 4
Imagination and Vision

Imagination and Vision

Opening Invocation

Imagination and vision are your great friends. Claim your ability to reach into the depths of your stored knowledge, gifts, and talents to create something that has never been seen or experienced before. Use your deep gift for building relationships to foster connections and creativity. Play, dance, and sing to remind yourself that imagination is not something generated in static isolation.

Opening Ideas for Contemplation

The possible's slow fuse is lit by
the imagination.
— Emily Dickinson

Everything you can imagine is real.
— Pablo Picasso

Vision is the art of seeing what is invisible
to others.
— Jonathan Swift

Vision looks inward and becomes duty.
Vision looks outward and becomes
aspiration. Vision looks upward and
becomes faith.
— Stephen S. Wise

Introduction to Imagination

The feminine brain thinks in flexible ways. We build relationships through our web of interconnectedness, and thus we have the capacity to imagine and create connections between people, places, and things that have not yet been identified or discovered. After all, what is imagination but the ability to reach into the depths of one's stored knowledge, experience, skills, and talents to create new ways of being and new visions for our lives?

Imagination is the source of creativity and feeds the soul. It thrives in a spirit of lightness and play, and it is fed by joy, fun, and laughter. When we daydream, imagine, fantasize, and envision, we explore a world without boundaries, where everything is connected, and anything is possible. This world is available to us each and every day, for we are the creators of the world of our imagination. Our imagination and ability to envision form the lens through which we see our daily world, a lens that generates our daily experience.

We have a far greater say in how we imagine, envision, and create our world than we think. It is through our beliefs that our world is created. Our belief in our own power to imagine, envision, and shape reality holds the promise needed to create the world of prosperity and equality that is needed today. Indeed, there has never been a time in the history of the world where imagination and vision have been more greatly needed than they are now, for the systems of the past are breaking down. This breakdown is apparent in our political and military defense systems and our attitudes and insensitivity towards the environment. And it is glaringly obvious in the lives of the many impoverished and disease-ridden peoples across our globe.

Great opportunities now exist for new ideas and imagination to be expressed: we stand in front of the doorway to building new systems that include equality and compassion as core values. We are in the process of a reconstruction that will require crisp imagination and visionary thinking. Women are needed in the fields of science and technology, in order to create technologies that will reverse the damage we have done to our planet, protect the health of those who are voiceless, and create safety and equality where none currently exists. We are faced today with the challenge of imagining a world where we can live in peace, with fairness and equality.

It has become essential for us as women to find solutions at a local level—in our own communities and families. We must use our feminine strengths in the areas of vision and imagination, start at home with ourselves, our families, and our communities, and create places of care and promise. We then must use our imagination and vision to picture a world of care and promise, taking action to build a bridge from our daily reality to one in which the needs of our world are fulfilled.

Recreating our world is totally possible, but it will require us to picture the world as we wish it to be, to share our vision with others, and, finally, to take small steps each day to create balance and wholeness.

Inspiring Questions

1. Where does your imagination most strongly live?

2. Is your imagination fully expressed in your life?

3. Describe your vision for a life and world with hope, promise, and equity. What is the first thing you need to do to bring this vision to life?

Witnessing

Picture your days filled with experiences that bring you the greatest joy and happiness. Make a commitment to expand your imagination and vision to include your own life, lived in a way that expresses what you value and care for the most. If possible, be witnessed by a friend or someone who supports you.

Maureen Simon

Imagination and Vision from the Feminine Perspective

About imagination and vision

Imagination is the gift that allows us to pluck ideas from the knowledge we have gained over time, assemble reams of information in new ways, and explore how various combinations play out. It is believed that the ability to imagine arises from the prefrontal cortex of the brain (Fisher 22), where patterns are assimilated, plans made, and novel responses generated. Because the female brain has a highly developed prefrontal cortex and our brain circuitry is highly connected, we are likely to access the imagination with greater ease than the male.

It may also be said that women's ease with imagination and vision stems from our early comfort with imaginary play—the fairy world, our love of tea parties, our ability to create alternate worlds, and so forth. If we choose to remember these childhood experiences, we can access and apply our natural comfort in those areas to freeing our imagination in today's adult world.

Why imagination and vision are unique to the feminine

The feminine brain has a natural ability for web-centered thinking. This includes her ability to access

her intuition, think in flexible ways, and have a long-term perspective. These gifts can be applied actively in doing business, evaluating the state of the world, and reaching all the decisions we make in our daily lives.

How women can use our gifts of imagination and vision

Since women have the natural ability to envision the whole, it is we who will now be called upon to envision a new world in a whole new way. Acting from our strength as deliverers and protectors of life, we can imagine no other world than one where life is created and maintained with respect and honor. It is the feminine that is now being called forth to create and hold a new vision. We must take the lead and step into this role, using all of our natural talents, gifts, and abilities. Our imagination is the key to our future.

Why imagination and vision are needed in the world now

At the time of this writing, there are 31 violent conflicts across the globe. Clearly we are in a position to reshape the history to come using the attributes and gifts of the feminine, for the future desperately needs our perspective. It is particularly important today to look at some of these ridiculous, meaningless conflicts, inequalities, and power games and then imagine what else could be. Due to the capabilities of the female brain and women's ability to be compassionate and concerned for the whole, the feminine is the natural leader to move us through the blockages and old ways that the world currently embraces.

Remember imagination and vision when...

...you hear something in the daily news that disturbs you, witness the birth of a baby, or take in the beauty of a sunset. Remember that your imagination holds the potential to recreate our current blueprint. Imagine.

Enlivening imagination and vision in your life

Notice where your imagination spontaneously leads you. Remember that imagination is informed by your stored knowledge, the history you embody, and the curiosity you have about new ways of being. Allow yourself to witness areas where you see a need for change and listen to the small voice within for guidance in knowing whether or not this is an area of significance to you. Begin to notice the parts of your life in which your imagination provides you with ideas and information. Follow these paths. They may lead you to some surprising places and provide great benefit to others.

Chapter 5
Creativity and Innovation

Creativity and Innovation

Opening Invocation

As the bearers of life, women are deeply connected to the creative process of generating something new, which changes our reality, world view, and ability to impact our experience. As expressed through women's many crafts and artistic pursuits, creativity and innovation generate solutions, beauty, and harmony in our world. We can use our flexible brains to guide the innovation that the world now deeply needs. Our creativity is an added source for our power and contribution.

Opening Idea for Contemplation

> *The significant problems we face today*
> *cannot be solved at the same level of thinking*
> *we were at when we created them.*
> *–Albert Einstein*

Introduction to Creativity and Innovation

One of the gifts of the feminine is our ability to remain creative while swimming upstream against the critical obstacles that we face. We have a sense of tenacity that allows us to create and offer our contributions in challenging times. The structure of our brain predisposes us to abundant creativity—due to our advanced, evolved intuition, linguistic skills, and

cerebral development—which can be seen in our ability to think flexibly. Since we are the ultimate vessels for the creation of life, we naturally embody the role of overseer for the protection, safety, and common good of all.

Most creative women are more interested in the intrinsic value of their contribution than the fame and power it may bring them. They often experience their creative offerings as another form of interconnecting, collaborating, and sharing. Indeed, it is not always necessary for the feminine to distinguish itself or set itself apart. Often creative experiences emerge from many minds, where one person does not hold all the answers or create all the breakthroughs.

Our world today greatly needs the feminine attributes to be fundamental in generating new forms of thought for peacemaking, creating egalitarian societies, and protecting our environment. Women are uniquely poised to offer creative solutions that will eliminate the need for control over natural resources. Our role as caretaker allows us to consider the needs of all when making critical global decisions. It will be an ideal world when gender is not a barrier to full expression, women share the helm of science and technology with men, and the masculine and feminine together create and refashion the direction of our world.

Inspiring Questions

1. How can you use your creativity and inspiration in your daily life?

2. What form does your creativity most naturally take?

3. How can you use your creativity to improve your life and the life of one other person?

Witnessing

Make a commitment to explore your greatest creative strengths. Decide one way that you can bring more creativity into your life. If possible, be witnessed by a friend or someone who supports you.

Creativity and Innovation

About creativity and innovation

In the world of the feminine, creativity and innovation stem from our ability to perceive the creative process as interconnected and interdependent. In many cases, women are more interested in the inherent value of their creations than in any fame or power that might accrue from them. Always inclusive, feminine creativity allows for and respects the thoughts and contributions of many—which enhances the overall creative process.

Why creativity and innovation are unique to the feminine

The structure of the female brain functions well in an environment that is predisposed to creativity; mental flexibility, intuition, and advanced linguistic facilities are a few examples of feminine gifts that support advanced creative expression. If we assume that women also have the ability to create that comes from holding a broad, contextual, long-term perspective—which enhances our depth and breadth of vision—it stands to reason that this ability allows us to see things holistically. This holistic view gives women the ability to innovate and create with more resources than we would otherwise have. By our very nature as the ones who give birth, women serve as the ultimate vessels for creativity. Women's creativity is diverse and central to life.

How women can use our gifts of creativity and innovation

The current world demands innovation, creativity, and fast information exchange. The female brain is wired to deliver these qualities. Women's natural ability to foster positive relationships encourages interdependence, which leads to positive, successful outcomes. When combined with our mental flexibility, imagination, and advanced verbal abilities, women excel.

Why creativity and innovation are needed in the world now

As it currently exists, the world favors a situation in which power and wealth are in the hands of approximately 20 percent of the population. This has created a paradigm of haves and have-nots and is counterintuitive to the feminine's natural desire to be inclusive and care for the whole. Innovation and new design are needed in all our cultures worldwide, for we must answer the following questions to build a world that is more harmonious and integrated than it is today. How can we feed the children? What will it take to stop the spread of the hundreds of deadly diseases? What innovation is needed for us to create sustainability among all cultures of the world, and how can the most powerful nations lead and nurture others

in this venture? How can we communicate with each other to fashion peace as we learn each other's cultures and build understanding?

These questions can best be answered when the feminine is included, for the feminine is naturally wired to create new solutions and innovations that may solve all the world's problems, concerns, and issues.

Remember your creativity and innovation when...

...an idea comes to mind as a flash, divination, or intellectual thought. Notice the ideas that you have, and which ideas are innovative and creative. How can you move forward with these ideas without inhibition? Where would these ideas best serve you and the world? What do you need now to realize them in the world and make them a reality? Don't play small: ask for support and then proceed.

Enlivening creativity and innovation in your life

Place yourself near beauty. Walk in nature. Notice the feelings, observations, or thoughts come up. Do more of the things that you love. Nurture yourself. Steep yourself in silence. Make sure to charge your soul, and be very clear about exactly what does charge your soul. Build time into your day for this nurturance. Make time for reflection. Do what excites you.

Chapter 6
Language

Language

Opening Invocation

When the feminine speaks, she often seeks to encourage connection and cooperation. She builds on similarities and likenesses to strengthen relationships. She encourages the sharing of feelings, thoughts, and personal stories to build mutual respect, care, and concern. She richly expresses the many facets of an issue, as she searches for deep, satisfying solutions.

Opening Idea for Contemplation

> *Thinking cannot be clear until it has had*
> *expression. We must write, or speak, or*
> *act our thoughts, or they will remain in a*
> *half torpid form. Our feelings must have*
> *expression, or they will be as clouds, which,*
> *till they descend in rain, will never bring up*
> *fruit or flower. So it is with all the inward*
> *feelings; expression gives them development.*
> *Thought is the blossom; language the*
> *opening bud; action the fruit behind it.*
> *– H.W. Beecher*

Introduction to Language

In the feminine style of communicating, conversations are negotiations for seeking and giving confirmation and support—a forum for reaching consensus.

When a group of women meet, the first item on the agenda is often complimenting each other and building a conversation around similarities, shared knowledge, and shared connections. This levels the playing field, builds trust, and provides an opening for further exploration and connection. Building trust and relationships through the use of language is central to the feminine, for when we develop trust and make connections, we establish that we are of equal status. This equal status or resonance is the foundation for building deep relationships, and it begins in the initial phase of conversations.

The feminine responds best when her feelings are validated through communication. It is important to her that she feel seen, heard, and acknowledged. She does this by sharing troubles and joys, and also information about what is happening in her life. Emotional connection and communication go hand in hand for the feminine and bring her from the invisible to the visible. Numerous studies have shown that women have 11 percent more brain neurons than men, which results in superior emotional expression and greater memory of emotional events than most men have.

The masculine style of communication tends to be more linear, abstract, and emotionally unexpressive compared to that of the feminine. In fact, when the two styles meet, there is often a chasm that needs to be bridged. In the masculine world, the need for this emotional expressivity is often questioned. In the feminine world, however, life is more than just achieving a goal: the richness of life includes memories of details and events. To the feminine, it is important that life be a qualitative, colorful, and dynamic experience. Our style of communication supports and expresses these values.

Inspiring Questions

1. How do you encourage connection and cooperation in your conversations?

2. How can you begin to share greater mutual respect for others through your listening and speaking?

3. Where is your communication most descriptive and alive? How could you further develop this aliveness?

Witnessing

Notice how you speak based on the reading about the attribute of language. If this is an area where you feel you need to gain strength, make a commitment. If possible, be witnessed by a friend or someone who supports you.

Connection and Cooperation

About connection and cooperation

The feminine has a natural ability to use language to express deep feelings, observations, thoughts, and concerns. She makes her emotions clear through language. For her, conversations are an opportunity to seek information and give confirmation and support. They also allow the feminine to negotiate and to reach consensus—two central values that lead her towards harmony and peacemaking. Through her advanced ability to communicate and express herself, connection and cooperation become natural assets and outcomes.

Why connection and cooperation are unique to the feminine

Women value collaborating and bridging differences. We build this connection and cooperation by emphasizing our similarities and equal status as we share knowledge. The creation of this equal playing field helps even the score and provides an inviting, safe environment. Women have the ability to express a message of support rather than disdain through tone of voice and selection of words. We also understand that an apology is not a sign of weakness but rather a sign of strength that makes room for cooperation and collaboration. By being willing to apologize, women level the playing field.

Maureen Simon

How women can use our gifts of connection and cooperation

Since women naturally focus on connection, by nature we downplay differences, using consensus and support to build strong relationships. The feminine prioritizes these two qualities, understanding that life is not a zero-sum contest nor that there always has to be a winner. The masculine has a natural tendency to work to achieve the upper hand, whereas the feminine works to achieve equality. By minimizing the importance of competition and winning, the feminine builds connections and bridges between people, as opposed to the disharmony inherent in the zero-sum model. This does not mean that all women are uncompetitive, as many enjoy sports and relish individual accomplishment. Our current world has encouraged women to adapt to a masculine, competition-based model and to become increasingly competitive in order to fit in and succeed. As women gain confidence about our natural gifts in the areas of connection and cooperation, we will be in an increasingly stronger position to lead, construct bridges, and encourage harmony.

Why connection and cooperation are needed in the world now

Given that we are all on this planet together, each voice needs to be heard fully, because every individual's life decisions affect all of us. Coming from a perspective of connection and equal status, the feminine

seeks to create trust, for it is the bedrock that supports creativity, productivity, and self-expression. Since the world is often perceived as competitive and harsh, we now need increased understanding. We must all look outside of ourselves, be inclusive, and show full respect for different points of view. The feminine invites connection and cooperation through her natural grace and concern for all.

Remember connection and cooperation when...

...you are in a situation where you can see that situational dynamics are creating conflict, disharmony, or pain. At that point, say something to move the situation to a more peaceful outcome than might otherwise be possible. Speak from your wisdom. Notice what information is missing. Use your intuition and your keen ability to observe body language, emotion, and tone. At those times in your personal life when you notice yourself avoiding conflict because of a natural desire to maintain harmony, figure out new ways to speak and to express what is most important to you.

Enlivening connection and cooperation in your life

Whenever you can, use supportive words, phrases, and ideas. Notice how your overall language brings people towards you or pushes them away. Notice whether your communication is clear enough. Could it be clearer? If you are getting feedback in your

day-to-day life, take note of it. When you are able to create powerful, clear conversations that reflect your thoughts and feelings and help you connect deeply with another person, you will have achieved mastery of this attribute.

Emotional Expressivity

About emotional expressivity

Connection is paramount for women; we connect by sharing feelings, information, and personal events. As noted above, the female brain has 11 percent more neurons than men, a greater neuronal capacity that supports superior emotional expression and increased memory of emotional events (Brizendine 5; Fisher 61, 94). Women are known to be more acute than men in our attention to visual, spatial, and verbal detail, which carries through to our accuracy in authentic and specific emotional and verbal expression. Women also understand the importance of validating others through communication, as we, ourselves, respond positively when our feelings are validated.

Why emotional expressivity is unique to the feminine

When emotional connection and communication are lacking, we feel invisible. When we engage in emotionally expressive conversations, we create valuable connections that allow us to feel understood and part of something bigger than ourselves. Furthermore, emotionally expressive conversations are easier to remember than flat ones: there are increased cues to aid recall, connection, and sharing, all of which deepen relationships and invite intimacy and understanding. Women comprehend the risk of vulnerability inherent in emotional sharing, but we know that it is a risk worth taking in order to reap the rewards of increased connection and relationship. Often when I speak to women they speak of dissatisfaction with men's silence and selective listening. I believe that both masculine socialization and brain structure support the development of these communication styles. We now must build bridges of awareness for masculine and feminine communication to evolve to a higher level of understanding.

How women can use our gift of emotional expressivity

Women need to express their feelings in order to be seen, heard, and acknowledged. When we allow ourselves to be open and vulnerable, we provide others with the opportunity to do the same. This openness results in a more authentic and deeper level of communication than would otherwise be possible. If we communicate on a deep level, sharing secrets and emotions, we will not feel alone in the world. In other words, connecting to others is at the heart of friendship and community building. This advanced style of communication challenges us to risk showing our vulnerability—especially in business and public environments. Despite the risk, it has become necessary for the feminine to lead in this arena, raising the bar so that authentic communication will become the norm.

Why emotional expressivity is needed in the world now

When people's diverse needs are taken into consideration, the result is higher, more meaningful participation by everyone than otherwise happens. Such a holistic, inclusive approach enriches the experiences and quality of life for all and creates a world of mutual respect. Mutual respect opens lines of communication, resulting in rich, full dialogues and exchanges. When women truly understand the special, unique gift of their emotional expressivity, we will gain a new level of self-respect and self-value, encouraging everyone—both men and women— to live and express themselves from a higher level of truth than when less authentic communication takes place. Generally speaking, when emotions are encouraged and enlivened in our daily communication and life, women feel alive and passionate. This leads us to increase our sense of value and respect for our own lives and the lives of others.

Remember emotional expressivity when...

...you are communicating with someone and notice that you are speaking in a linear and overly concise manner in order to fit into the conversation. Make a decision to speak in a communication style that is more authentic to you as you blend your speaking with your co-communicator's ability to listen. The art is to find a balance that allows you to express your observations, opinions, and wisdom so that the listener can still participate and benefit from the conversation.

Enlivening emotional expressivity in your life

Your emotions inform what feels good and bad/right and wrong to you. Notice your emotions on a daily basis. Use them as guides, not rulers. Include your emotions and feelings when you speak. Find a way to communicate that expresses the richness of what you feel, and open the conversation to include and receive the emotions and richness of others.

Verbal Agility

About verbal agility

The female brain has developed a high aptitude for verbal agility. Because feminine communication is more descriptive than that of the masculine and uses story and metaphor, this creates an opportunity for more people to relate to a given conversation and to feel included, which allows people to connect on a deeper level, with more clarity than they might have with linear communication. Women's interest in the many facets of an issue opens up discussion, expands what is under consideration, and leads to the formation of rich solutions.

Why verbal agility is unique to the feminine

The ability to develop, design, and construct concepts and ideas that can be deeply heard and understood allows for meaningful communication. When we hold the gift of verbal agility, we have available to us a wide array of means that can enhance clarity and understanding. Verbal agility is both a gift and an art, in that it opens doors and allows us to walk through those doors with a rich experience of life, to understand and connect to others who have different experiences from ours, and to make room for new relationships to emerge.

How women can use our gift of verbal agility

Given that the masculine and feminine clearly have different styles of communication, it is now time for the feminine to make her style of communicating known and valued. As we become increasingly free in speaking with a circular, agile, and expressive form of communication, women will gain acceptance of our speaking style in the world of business and in life.

If we are aware that our verbal agility is a gift and an art, we will stand behind our gift, teach that gift to our daughters, and own it with a sense of pride. Concise, quick, clear, masculine communication—using few words—has become the norm in our business world and life. Yet so much is missed when things are said quickly and in haste. The feminine holds the ability to slow language down and to bring forth words and conversations that make time for and create clear and meaningful dialogue.

Why verbal agility is needed in the world now

Verbal agility is a skill or gift that offers the opportunity for enhanced and meaningful conversations. As women speak up and feel increasingly confident, they will then move into increasingly relevant positions of leadership and contribution on the world stage of business, politics, and life. It is through conversation and dialogue—not war and aggression—that the world will find equilibrium and harmony, and move towards a state of peace. The richer our expression and the more descriptive the discussion of the many facets of an issue, the greater the opportunity for creating a clear, rich solution.

Verbal agility is a necessary skill that the world now cries out for as we attempt to build understanding and connection. It is one of the most important attributes needed to create a world of compassion and peace.

Remember your verbal agility when...

...your clarity of thought is needed to enhance or contribute to a conversation, decision, policy, or project. Organize your thoughts clearly so that minds that are more linear than yours can accept your clear, concise words as a major contribution to the dialogue. Value any strength that you have in the area of verbal agility, as it is through verbal agility that great changes can be described and realized.

Enlivening verbal agility in your life

Notice where your communication is most outstanding! Build on it. Notice where your communication could be enhanced! Develop it. Find excitement in the creative ways in which you are able to speak and communicate. Support a young girl or another woman in noticing and building her own strengths, gifts, and talents in this area. Join a local speaking group to

support yourself in developing this skill further if you are called upon to speak in public. There is great help available to enable you to strengthen your voice. Call upon it.

Nonverbal communication

About nonverbal communication

Most women would agree that they can walk into a room and identify the emotions and moods of others via both body language and intuition. Tonal range also provides vast amounts of information to women and leads to exchanges with increased sensitivity and understanding. The feminine gleans information as she hears the tone of voice and demeanor in a conversation. This provides her with a heightened sense of awareness. This attribute is not specific to the feminine, but her memory and depth of connection are greater than those of the masculine due to her highly developed, dominant right brain, which registers experiences in technicolor (Brizendine 13).

Why nonverbal communication is unique to the feminine

Anthropological research shows us that female monkeys produce a larger array of whimpers, coos, and barks than male monkeys do. These have been interpreted as "middle-range social" calls (tones used to encourage connectivity). Since we learn and have been socialized from our early ancestors—both human and animal—it can be assumed that women have acquired the brain circuitry for a more intricate tonal range than men (Fisher 64). Other research shows us that women's voices are more variable, musical, and expressive than men's voices. Because the right hemisphere tends to be dominant in the female brain, feelings and experiences are recorded in vivid detail and can be fully explored. And because the right hemisphere of the brain rules creativity and emotions, the female brain has strong access to feelings as well.

How women can use our gift of nonverbal communication

Knowing that we can read faces, are sensitive to body language, and have an innate gift of tuning into more intricate and wider tonal ranges than men, we can now claim our capability to use these talents to perceive and understand the environments in which we live with a profound understanding. The swift speed of our lives today sometimes moves us away from our ability to connect with another deeply. If we can take time to pay attention and to notice others' presence and what their bodies are telling us, we can more accurately interpret and influence a given situation or set of needs than we otherwise might, and, as a result, enrich our level of understanding and connection—as well as arriving at a better outcome for all involved.

Why nonverbal communication is needed in the world now

The world we live in moves quickly, as it focuses on accountability and outcome. We must connect more

deeply and more sensitively with others than has typically been the case, in order for us to build a world that encompasses care, compassion, and understanding. The feminine's advanced gifts of understanding intricate tonal ranges and reading faces, emotions, and body language place her in the role of teaching others the arts of engagement, sensitivity, and full participation in relationships with others. Nonverbal cues provide women with invaluable information with which we can work towards building deep relationships and great understanding.

Remember nonverbal communication when...

...you enter a room and need to gather information at a deep, sensitive level that will inform you about your environment. Remember that your ability to communicate without speech is a unique and special talent that you can use in combination with your intuition. Used together, these two gifts can lead you to an advanced level of understanding. Employ these talents to make a difference and a contribution. Remember to go beyond the words that you hear. At times, the messages expressed silently are far deeper and much more meaningful than those expressed with words.

Enlivening nonverbal communication in your life

Experiment with your ability to enter a room and observe what is going on without speaking a word. Notice the tones you hear, the body language you see, and the general feeling you sense in a room. This observational mode will allow you to become more astute and aware of your overall environment. Notice your own silent communications. What messages are you sending? How are you being received? What does your body language express about you? Much knowledge and information can be gleaned in silence. Verbal communication is only one part of the message we send. Picture a world in which all of your natural gifts and abilities are used to read the world around you and to gain and communicate a greater understanding of it.

Part III:
Aligning Power, Intuition, and Beauty from the Feminine Perspective

Chapter 7
Beauty and Aesthetics

Beauty and Aesthetics

Opening Invocation

The feminine has a heightened sensitivity to and awareness of physical beauty and aesthetics. Beauty and aesthetics build connections—to others, our environment, and the richness and experiences life has to offer. They bring us out of ourselves and link us to things far greater than our individual lives and regular surroundings.

The feminine tends to live in the moment and experience spirit and matter as one, paying close attention to the relationship between the intangible (the sensed/the unseen) and the physical. When our environment and our internal experiences are in harmony with each other, our being reflects the graceful beauty and sense of aesthetics that the feminine is uniquely able to offer. And, when we are able to find beauty in all areas of our life, we are more open to experiencing the beauty of our own nature. Thus, our connection to beauty is essential.

There are many angles from which to view and explore beauty. For example, understanding that the feminine ability to create and perceive beauty is unique and important, offers most women a powerful perspective — they must realize and claim. Some women already know that beauty is food for the soul: they live with this value at the center of each day. Ideally, though,

I wish that realization to reach all women—and that all women worldwide can live securely in the knowledge that beauty is important and firmly linked to the feminine.

Opening Idea for Contemplation

The Beautiful stirs passion and urgency in us and calls us forth from aloneness into the warmth and wonder of some eternal embrace. It unites us again with the neglected and forgotten grandeur of life. The call of beauty is not a cold call into the dark or the unknown; in some instinctive way, we know that beauty is no stranger. We respond with delight to the call of beauty because in an instant it can awaken under the layers of the heart some forgotten brightness.

– John O'Donohue

 Maureen Simon

Introduction to Beauty and Aesthetics

Defining Beauty and Aesthetics

Arriving at a definition for beauty has confounded philosophers throughout the centuries. If we look up the formal definition of beauty and aesthetics from the Merriam Webster Dictionary, we read:

> ***Beauty**—the quality or aggregate of qualities in a person or thing that gives pleasure to the senses or pleasurably exalts the mind or spirit.*
>
> ***Aesthetics**—a pleasing appearance or effect.*

From these two definitions, we can see that pleasure is a direct outcome of beauty and aesthetics.

I believe that the feminine embodies beauty at its highest frequency. We all experience beauty from the internal response it elicits, and, in a sense, we can measure beauty by the emotion(s) and feeling(s) we experience in its presence. In this way, beauty allows us to experience feelings that we would otherwise not be able to access without its presence in our lives. Women's heightened attention to the details in their environment, as well as their awareness of the impact that these details have on the quality of experiences leads them towards a deep connection to their environment and the beauty of the world. While less

attuned to beauty than the feminine, the masculine is nevertheless drawn to the feminine, by nature.

There are many perspectives from which to view the subject of beauty. If you research "feminine beauty" on the internet, for example, you are likely to find a series of articles and discussions on "how to be/become beautiful." This, however, is not what interests me. Instead, I am interested in looking at the way women and the feminine have a natural and direct affinity for and connection to beauty and the aesthetic in the world. And I am interested in exploring how the feminine receives, creates and is sensitive to beauty in the environment and how her heightened sense of and connection to beauty enriches life and benefits us all.

Beauty connects and inspires diverse worlds. It has long been a magnetic attractor that brings people together across values, religions, and geography. Extensive cultural exchanges exist to provide us with opportunities to learn about the best of ourselves and others, through the expression of beauty in the worlds of art, architecture, design, nature, and the rich variety of music and fashion across peoples and cultures. All of these mediums inspire and engage both the imagination and pleasure.

Throughout history, the feminine has sought to create environments via personal expressions that enhance comfort, beauty, and pleasure. Women have a unique connection to beauty that often allows us to experience our bodies, nature, and the physical world in a full, intense, and dynamic way. We speak of perceiving beauty while experiencing states of grace, peace, harmony, sensitivity, visual elation, and divine connection.

Inspiring Questions

1. How do you describe beauty?

2. Is there beauty in your inner and outer life?

3. Where could you bring more beauty into your daily experience?

4. How can you make changes in your home and work environment to reflect your own unique sense of beauty more accurately than it is currently expressed?

Witnessing

Make a commitment to enhance the beauty in your life. Notice where in your life you currently experience the most beauty and then give yourself the space and time in your life to include more of it. Clarify for yourself how and where your life might benefit if more beauty were present. Commit to honoring this need. If possible, be witnessed by a friend or someone who supports you.

Appreciation of Beauty and Aesthetics

About the appreciation of beauty and aesthetics

Across most cultures, women—with their feminine attributes and gifts—have been the creators of beauty in dwellings and other areas of life. In most cultures women create homes and design safe, secure and nurturing environments for their children, family and friends—environments that support the development and growth of the individual and build connection to spirit, the source of all beauty.

In and of itself, beauty is neither masculine nor feminine. But in comparison to the masculine, the feminine more often prioritizes beauty in the midst of daily life. In other words, for the feminine, beauty is often a core value and key attribute. In general, most people say that when they look at a flower, a landscape or a sky full of floating clouds they are experiencing their feminine side. This feeling of appreciating something intangibly beautiful is difficult to put into words—but it is clearly a part of our feminine nature.

Beauty offers us an experience that can elicit a unique, deep peace and harmony unlike anything else. It provides a sense of elation that can involve any and all of the senses. Beauty often evokes tranquility, much like what one feels when in nature or in a physically beautiful human-built environment.

With her awareness of aesthetics, the feminine is often interested in creating beauty in the spaces in which she works and lives. She places objects in such a way that they elevate the ordinary to the artistic, and with her ability to pay close attention to details, she can create amazing environments.

Why the appreciation of beauty and aesthetics is unique to the feminine

Our relationship to a beautiful object or form begins with perception. This perception leads us to experience the spirit of the form or object from within ourselves, a connection that ultimately touches our soul and allows us to experience beauty fully. As previously mentioned, the feminine experiences beauty based on her internal response, often on an emotional, feeling level. Thus, since women are in close, immediate contact with their emotions, they also have a readily available connection and access to beauty. Women have this unique connection to beauty as they perceive the external—nature and the world—and the internal—their bodies and their spirits—intensely and as one.

Women are the givers of life through the birth process, which makes them deeply connected and highly sensitized to all life. This increased sensitivity and awareness gives women deep and immediate access to beauty. As co-creators of life, women also have an enhanced capacity to experience and perceive their surroundings.

Women's feminine nature gives them the ability to create, nurture, and nourish life, so that it flourishes and grows. The feminine's ability to mother—to encourage life to thrive—goes far beyond the individual creatures and forms that she herself has given birth to. Her ability to nurture is instinctive, related to all the lives she touches. This very nurturance is, itself, a form of beauty.

I believe that the feminine's connection with—and heightened awareness of—Beauty and the Aesthetics exists in at least four distinct areas:

~ Beauty and the senses;

~ Beauty and harmony;

~ Beauty as nourishment;

~ Beauty, awe and appreciation.

Beauty and the Senses

Through our five senses—i.e., hearing, sight, smell, touch and taste—we learn about our environment and gain an understanding of our world. Our connection with beauty heightens our sensory awareness. It is time for us to increase our awareness of our senses— to work to decrease any desensitization—and build a stronger relationship with beauty than we now have. Increasing our connection to beauty increases our connection to the divine, the source of all beauty.

Since the feminine experiences beauty from the inside out—i.e., from how her perception within interacts with her environment without—she is able to feel all aspects of her environment and appreciate it greatly. When women begin to realize that the feminine has a particularly strong connection to and understanding of beauty and the aesthetic, our confidence in ourselves will increase, as will our pleasure in all sensory areas.

In today's world, we move quickly—often far too quickly. We would often benefit by slowing down, so that we can pay attention to the powerful information and experiences that our senses constantly provide us about the beauty surrounding us.

Beauty and Harmony

Beauty can provide us with a sense of elation, for it offers us a harmonious, unparalleled experience of peace. As noted, the feminine's sensitivity to beauty often leads her to want to create beauty. The cycle is self-perpetuating: beauty inspires us; when we see or experience something beautiful, we gain a sense of harmony. In other words, beauty leads to harmony, then harmony back to beauty. Likewise, when we listen to a beautiful piece of music or see a beautiful garden where the plants harmoniously blend together to create a beautiful tapestry, we are experiencing a powerful blessing, a gift that increases our internal sense of peace.

In her essay, "Truth and Beauty," Eva Peck reminds us of the connection between natural harmony and beauty:

> *Like in a beautiful symphony, there is harmony throughout the natural world. Interdependence and cooperation occur everywhere. The many different life forms and natural cycles are intertwined and balanced (barring unwise human intervention)... Not only is everything in the natural world balanced and functional, but beauty also surrounds us. Consider the harmony of the colors. Splashes of red, yellow, orange, pink, purple, and brown add interest as well as promoting feelings of cheer, serenity, inspiration, and vitality, among others. The natural beauty, aesthetically pleasing to the senses, brings happiness, enjoyment, and even amusement.*

Beauty as Nourishment

There is beauty in the simplest form of nourishment, in a meal that provides comfort and sustains life. Beauty also exists in the grace and bounty of the earth's minerals, air, water, and harvest. As a result, it comes as no surprise that the earth has been regarded as "feminine" by writers and authors throughout history, nor that our beautiful, bounteous planet is commonly referred to as" Mother Earth" for the nurturing and stable care she gives us all.

While beauty nourishes the body, it also feeds the mind, soul and heart. Indeed, it could be argued that if we only nourish the body but starve the soul, we have, nonetheless, still starved the whole being. Thus, the feminine's attention to beauty is yet another way in which she feeds and nourishes those around her— as well as herself.

The feminine has a special way of elevating the ordinary to the artistic, an ability that derives from her close attention to details. What makes something mundane? What turns the mundane into an artistic or even sublime expression of beauty? Often the difference is subtle and dwells in the small, specific, and absolutely crucial details. A mere step away from the mundane, the most sublime beauty enriches, nourishes and feeds all who experience it.

When women learn to open ourselves to receiving all the goodness and beauty of the world, we make a regular practice of experiencing life with pleasure, filling and nourishing our soul until it is replete with beauty and contentment.

Beauty, Awe and Appreciation

Women's perception of beauty connects us to our world and the cosmos. Beauty inspires us to feel awe and appreciation. These are subtle emotions, and they serve to enhance our connection to our hearts and our spirits, to our essence and true nature.

As I look out my window each day, I find myself inspired and in awe of the beauty in nature and the world. More and more in my life, I notice I find beauty, awe and appreciation whenever I seek it. I have started looking to find and experience the beauty in people and animals—and across all areas of my life. I firmly believe that beauty is there to be found: you just need to pay attention to it. One of my favorite sayings is, "Your energy follows wherever you place your attention." This is so easy to do—when speaking of beauty.

Most religious texts have quite a few references to beauty and awe, more specifically to awe inspired by beauty. Unsurprisingly, these two qualities are closely associated with a deep spiritual connection. One such reference, in this case speaking of modern Deist principles, is "You shall find awe, inspiration and beauty in the creation and the natural order of our world."

How women can use our gift of appreciation for beauty and aesthetics

As we begin to pay increased attention to beauty and aesthetics, we will automatically feel good about and enhance our experience of life. As we improve our sense of connection to our surroundings, we will also become more deeply connected to spirit than ever before. And as we claim the value of a heightened awareness of beauty and emotional perception, we will begin to live life more sensually and feel more alive than before. Beauty and the feminine connect us to our core selves and increase the quality of all areas of our lives.

Why the appreciation of beauty and aesthetics is needed in the world now

It is important to understand where the underlying desire for beauty stems from. Social scientists and psychologists consider beauty to be one of the few basic necessities for life. In fact, the American psychologist Abraham Maslow describes beauty, form and richness as core values that define one's being. In A Theory of Motivation (AM 1943), he notes that those who are self-actualized tend to incorporate more beauty than those who are not—along with other core values he describes—and he emphasizes that humans need to refresh themselves in the presence of beauty.

Looking across cultural lines, we find that anthropologists maintain that primitive people decorated their caves and adorned their bodies from the beginning of time. Beauty is, therefore, universal and the impulse towards beauty, eternal.

Beauty is a subjective experience. At its most profound, beauty can move us to reflect on the meaning of our own existence. This state of contemplation is essential, for our ability—and willingness—to contemplate the meaning of life is central to living a life of richness, depth, and contribution. In today's world, in which the time and energy for contemplation grows

progressively rarer and rarer, anything that provides an impulse towards reflection becomes increasingly precious. Beauty is a potent propellant.

So much has been written about beauty. As one example, the well known English philosopher, Alfred North Whitehead describes beauty in his Adventures in Ideas "not as mere ornamentation but as the central purpose of the universe." He extends his claim, saying that "beauty structures and directs the final aim of the universe" and that beauty "lies at the core of our lives and is a major part of our growth process. It informs us and teaches us through its unfolding presence." As a healthy plant and garden are beautiful; they bring with their presence alone–harmony, symmetry and balance.

Remember to appreciate beauty and aesthetics when...

...you are feeling full of life and have the gift of beauty to share with another. When you feel empty and devoid of beauty, take care to surround yourself with it. Know what is beautiful to you. Allow beauty to permeate every room in your physical environment, as well as your heart and mind. On a day when the world could be better than it appears, go out and seek beauty, for it is a direct connection to the divine. You will gain much strength and clarity from this connection, especially in times of need.

Enlivening the appreciation of beauty and aesthetics in your life

Bring flowers into your home; choose beautiful fabrics. Fill your refrigerator with beautiful and sensual foods, your ears with lovely sounds, your mind with beautiful readings, and your eyes with wonderful sights. Allow yourself to have quiet moments in your day in which you can notice the beauty that you normally would pass by.

Chapter 8
Intuition

Intuition

Opening Invocation

With our ability to tap into feelings, sense what is behind an emotion, keenly observe nonverbal cues, and receive information from the unseen, women have a natural ability to empathize, understand, and relate to others. Our intuition informs us through the physical, emotional, mental, and spiritual information that we receive. We excel in our ability to perceive far beyond what the eye can see. We use the gift of our intuition as a natural extension of our being, as it deeply guides how we live in the world.

Opening Ideas for Contemplation

> *A woman's guess is much more accurate*
> *than a man's certainty.*
> > *– Rudyard Kipling*

> *Intuition cannot be reduced to observation*
> *of behavior, body language, or other*
> *visual cues. It is a holistic awareness*
> *which includes both internal and external*
> *sensitivity and which sometimes transcends*
> *sensory input altogether.*
> > *– Helen Palmer, in Inner Knowing*

Introduction to Intuition

Intuition is a holistic awareness that includes our outer, external perceptions as well as our inner emotions and feelings. It is one of the most confusing gifts we own, because we receive it via different kinds of awareness. We often merge all types of intuition into one category, and, as a result, we find it challenging to explain our intuitive hits. If you are comfortable with your intuition, it can lead you towards clearer decisions and greater success than you would reach without it. For many women it is our guiding compass and greatest informer.

Part of the framework for this section is derived from my interpretation of the work of Frances Vaughn. Frances initially made me aware that intuition lives in four distinct areas: physical, emotional, mental, and spiritual. In the book *Inner Knowing* Frances writes:

> *The broad range of intuitive, human experiences falls into four distinct levels of awareness: physical, emotional, mental, and spiritual... Mystical experiences are intuitive experiences at the spiritual level and as such do not depend on sensory, emotional, or mental cues for their validity. Intuition at the physical level is associated with bodily sensations and at the emotional level with*

*feelings, and at the mental level with images
and ideas.*

From a biological perspective, women have a strong relationship between their intuitive hunches and their female biology. The section of the female brain that tracks intuitive feelings is larger and more sensitive than in the male brain. This leads women to understand that intuitive feelings or senses are not just emotional states, but that they are also related to physical sensations that are directly communicated to the brain. In addition, women are especially good at emotional mirroring; they have a well-developed ability to match breathing and posture and to serve as "human emotion detectors." This places women in a position to "mind-read," as our ability to observe and mirror another person activates similar brain patterns in the observer. The male brain triggers fewer intuitive sensations than the female brain—missing some of the emotional information—and is instead forced to lean more heavily on rational thought.

The world is in a state of fragmentation. Selective listening and the search for power have contributed to much of the unrest in he world that we currently face. The feminine is particularly well placed to create strong connections, take the bird's-eye view, and be concerned for the greater good of all. As we gradually increase our comfort level with our emotions and intuitive messages, we will learn that these are assets that can serve as guiding forces in our lives.

Inspiring Questions

1. How do physical cues enrich your intuitive understanding of others?

2. Where do you most find yourself trusting your inner voice?

3. How do your mind and your thought process inform your intuition?

Witnessing

Make a commitment to deepen your connection to your intuition. Notice where intuition lives in the physical, mental, emotional, and spiritual aspects of your life. Be aware of ways that you can begin to use your intuition with an increased level of trust. This may take time to slowly rebuild, as many of us have learned to listen and live from external cues and information alone and have lost touch with our natural sense of inner knowing. If possible, be witnessed and supported by a friend or someone who is comfortably and confidently using their intuition.

The Physical Intuitive Sense

About the physical intuitive sense

Intuition stems from the ability to call upon organized, stored expertise. Women are excellent at reading faces and processing small details about social interactions. This gift allows them to track the nuances in conversations and social settings, which then allows them more readily to intuit what is going on in their environment than men.

Why the physical intuitive sense is unique to the feminine

The areas of the female brain that track physical intuitive sensations are larger and more sensitive than in the male brain. In addition, with their well-connected left and right hemispheres of the brain, women are able to assimilate disparate facts and details more quickly than men. For the same reason, women think in the form of a web, looking at the whole and taking in information from all sources. As noted earlier, this capability is a gift that arises from activity in the connective tissue of the prefrontal cortex, which is more developed in women than men and is where the brain assembles and integrates information. "The prefrontal cortex directly connects the brain to other body circuits, in a process sometimes called body loops. These brain-body connections allow the women to have a gut reaction—which is often known as intuition." (Fisher 16)

How women can use our gift of the physical intuitive sense

Since we are often led by our minds, it is important for us to understand the more tangible, physical side of our gifts and talents. Research on the female brain has shown us that intuition is not airy-fairy and impractical, but rather rooted in our biology, and that we can have faith in intuition and call upon it in our daily lives as needed.

Why the physical intuitive sense is needed in the world now

As we are physical beings, our life force is informed by messages and information that come from the physical realm. Given that we are humans and live on the earth, the physical is a very important part of our makeup and presence. Therefore, it is essential that we take cues from our physical body: it can give us essential information. But it is also important to divide the physical aspect of intuition from the other three areas in which it operates (emotional, mental, and spiritual), because we have so much information coming to us through our senses. The physical cues of touch, sight, sound, taste, and smell all provide us with necessary information that feed and guide our intuitive, knowing perception of the world around us.

Using a combination of sources enriches the depth of our intuition.

Remember the physical intuitive sense when...

...you feel a sensation in your body that gives you a message or a sense of knowing, for at that moment you are in touch with your physical intuitive sense. Trust this information and use it when making a decision or taking action. Use your body as a compass or guide for gathering information about relationships, self-care, and life's general decisions. To do so, you must reach a certain level of trust and gain a certain level of experience in getting to know your physical intuitive sense. Practice, listen, and learn to trust.

Enlivening the physical intuitive sense in your life

Notice how you feel when you enter a room. What are the physical sensations that you experience with regards to the space and the general situation? Learn to rely on the physical cues that arise in different environments. Follow up information gleaned from your physical senses. Start to learn the signals that guide and inform you, so that you know the source of the information that you gain.

The Emotional Intuitive Sense

About the emotional intuitive sense

What we have commonly come to know as women's intuition exists first and foremost on the emotional level. Some people call this inner sense of knowing telepathy. Often it is said that women are more intuitive than men, which is based largely on the fact that women have not been forced into repressing their feelings as much as men. In early days of socialization, boys are often taught not to show emotions, while girls are given the message that being emotional is acceptable and even appropriate. This makes the emotional aspect of intuition more available to girls and women throughout their lives than to boys and men. Even though the left, rational side of the brain can easily take over the process of making decisions and judgments, our intuitive responses can still add emotional value.

Why the emotional intuitive sense is special to the feminine

In her ability to observe and imagine how another feels, the feminine brain activates brain patterns similar to those of the person she is in contact with. This is one of the highest forms of practicing empathy. The feminine holds great abilities for care and compassion, which are heightened by her emotional understanding of what another is feeling. This understanding comes from emotional intuition. Another reason why the intuitive sense in women is so keen is that ancestral women were constantly obligated to figure out the emotional needs of their pre-lingual, highly dependent young. This helped them develop somewhat of a sixth sense, enabling them to perceive and meet the needs of their young on both an emotional and physical level. This pattern recurs throughout history in the role of motherhood.

How women can use our gift of the emotional intuitive sense

One of the great secrets of intuition is women's apparent ability to read another person's mind (Brizendine 122). If you can understand and deeply empathize with how another feels, it allows for a deeper connection and understanding than you would otherwise have. When we can combine our strong, intuitive sense of knowing with perceiving and meeting the needs of others, we increase our level of contribution. And when we perceive and understand another's emotional needs, we can relate at a very deep level, opening doors for greater exchanges and more possibilities than we might have imagined.

Why the emotional intuitive sense is needed in the world now

For years women have been told that they are overly emotional and irrational. We have been weaned from trusting our small, inner voice and were told that its

knowledge was made up and inaccurate. After years of doubting our intuition, we have learned to detach our emotional sense of knowing from the world that we live in, creating a major disconnect for many women. It is time to regain our trust of our own inner voice, welcome the information provided by our emotions, and begin to seek guidance, knowledge, and wisdom from them.

Remember your emotional intuitive sense when...

...you begin to ignore the emotional cues that your body is giving you. Notice if someone else's voice is stronger than yours and makes you doubt something that you feel to be true in your own heart. Use this gift to feel into and deeply empathize with another, so that your connection can increase. Never block your emotions, nor let them run rampant, but use them for the guidance they provide. Use questions that stem from your intuitive hits to engage others in conversation and dialogue, as this will open doors and build understanding.

Enlivening the emotional intuitive sense in your life

In order to receive fully the powerful information that our intuition offers, we need to make space and create silence so that we can consciously connect with it. Meditation, silence, and intentional prayer are important ways to create an opening for which our intuition can develop. Meditation is very powerful as it allows us to connect deeply with the ever-present, higher dimensions that are available to us. In meditation, we slow down our normal thoughts and allow our higher self to inform us. We sometimes receive pictures or images and experience deep feelings. This stillness allows us to raise our energetic vibration to a higher frequency—as we are creatures made of energy and our vibration rises when we become clearer. As we practice stillness and meditation we will often notice an increased sensitivity and an open and sensitive way of experiencing the world.

The Mental Intuitive Sense

About the mental intuitive sense

Intuition plays a vital part in decision making, and the feminine values intuition greatly as part of her thinking process. The idea that the feminine is able to store experiences contributes to her intuitive thinking. As a result of his research, Herbert Simon (Carnegie-Mellon University) believed that intuition stems from the ability to call upon organized, stored expertise. Because women excel at reading faces and processing nuances of social interactions, they may well be better at intuiting the underlying elements of social exchanges than men are (Fisher 17-18).

Why the mental intuitive sense is special to the feminine

Women gather data on nuances and expressions, and they are superior to men at grouping and intuiting the subtleties of social interactions. Men pick up the subtle signs of sadness in a female face only 40 percent of the time, whereas women can pick up these signs 90 percent of the time (Brizendine 125). Our ability to gather these nuances into related groups allows us to spend more time focusing on important details, which can ultimately benefit all of our relationships. In addition, women consider the entire complexity of issues more accurately than men, which leads to more holistic, comprehensive, and often win-win worldviews and solutions. Women can approach

the world, as well as interactions, with more confidence than men when we utilize our intuitive mental gifts, as we have more information to support our interpretations.

How women can use our gift of the mental intuitive sense

By understanding the unique attributes and gifts that we have in the area of mental intuition, we can take a more holistic view than we otherwise would, as we utilize all the areas of our natural perception. When women begin to value our intuition fully as part of our thinking process, we begin to include and validate it as an important source of gathering information. We rely on our intuition and interpretive abilities to make decisions, basing them on images and concepts that link nonlinear information. When women are willing to accept the value of our intuitive senses, we can arrive at superior decisions more rapidly than would be possible in a rational, linear process.

Why the mental intuitive sense is needed in the world now

Mental intuition often involves openness to images, voices, and concepts that seem unrelated to the information at hand, but that draw our attention in a fruitful direction. Women are more accustomed than men to finding success when we follow our internal guidance through images and conceptual leaps. Men

tend to process information in an either/or way. They like to keep decisions simple and often do not include peripheral information (Frenier 24). Considering the complexities of the issues we face today, it is essential to include the holistic, comprehensive, integrated, and related view provided by women's mental intuitive sense. When we begin to value this powerful gift fully, the world will begin to value it as well.

Remember the mental intuitive sense when...

...you are with a male counterpart who begins to evaluate a situation in an either/or way—especially when you see the "gray" instead, as many women do. Know that seeing "gray," as opposed to black and white, is a natural gift and that your use of the right and left brain together with the body as a whole unit for perception provides rich and diverse answers and solutions.

Remember this attribute when you have a creative idea, intuitive hit, or thought that you feel you need to bring into the world. Never think that your ideas are too small or insignificant to speak of. Follow your intuition and allow your voice to be heard, for it is needed more now than ever. Don't play small: allow yourself to engage fully in your life and the world.

Enlivening the mental intuitive sense in your life

Take pride in the fact that your ability to consider all the complexities of an issue more accurately reflects the way the world actually works than a simplistic model. You have a holistic and comprehensive view available to you. Use it. Notice when your ability to see the whole can provide great insights. Notice when past stored experiences inform your current perceptions and intuition. Practice making decisions from an intuitive mental perception, as opposed to a strictly linear, rational viewpoint. If an image arrives when you are trying to make a decision, interpret it in light of your choice, and decide accordingly.

The Spiritual Intuitive Sense

About the spiritual intuitive sense

Spiritual intuition is a holistic perception of reality. In the spiritual sphere of intuition, we come to realize a great oneness—a sense of the interconnectedness of all. It is possible that we can become increasingly open and aware of mystical experiences, experiences that bring us out of our bodies into other realms, and, in the end, provide us with insights and wisdom that we begin to trust.

Of the four types of intuition, only the spiritual does not depend on sensory feedback, for it stands alone, informed by an inner sense of knowing. It transcends the usual, rational, dualistic way of knowing. Spiritual intuition provides us with a direct, transpersonal experience, which leads us to a deeper understanding of the source of our lives and our connection and awareness to all.

Why the spiritual intuitive sense is special to the feminine

Throughout the centuries, we find records of powerful female saints, goddesses, teachers, and healers who have had strong mystical experiences. The feminine is predisposed to these deep connections because we have more direct access than the masculine to the emotional side of the brain—the right side.

This access provides us with a strong sense of inter-connectedness and oneness, both of which stem from divine universal principles. Interconnection and one-ness stand at the gateway as beacons to the higher realms of consciousness.

How women can use our gift of the spiritual intuitive sense

When we begin to allow our intuition to guide us, the spiritual world speaks to us. Its messages, along with information that we would normally not see, feel, or experience, become available to us. We often move quickly past these informers in our active daily life. But when we make time for stillness and inner listen-ing through meditation, prayer, and contemplation, we open the gateway to another world. Divinations and synchronicities become abundant in our lives. The art is to trust messages, signs, and coincidences, and to act on them—if they call upon us to act. The more we listen and follow these subtle or sometimes not-so-subtle cues, the more we receive invaluable in-formation that can bring a whole new quality of living into our lives.

Why the spiritual intuitive sense is needed in the world now

Spiritual intuition stems from knowing that we live in a state of oneness, respecting all life. It is time to decide if we want to live our lives solely in our minds, seeking empirical evidence and confirmation, or if we

are ready to realize that something greater than our-selves—spirit—protects, guides, and informs all that we do. Tuning into our spiritual intuition allows us to receive information and guidance that enriches our lives and supports our growth on this earth.

So much of today's life is lived in the world of the mind and in the physical. It is almost as though we have forgotten, in the rush of things, the very source that informs our lives and the lives of everything around us. It is critical that we gain confidence in our spiritual intuition and inner sense of knowing, and begin to live, act, and be from that place.

Remember the spiritual intuitive sense when...

...you feel alone in the world and cut off from receiv-ing higher wisdom and knowledge. Remember this attribute when you are faced with challenging situa-tions in which you could benefit from receiving infor-mation to help you overcome the obstacles before you. Remember that you are never alone.

Enlivening the spiritual intuitive sense in your life

Meditation, prayer, friendship with like-minded souls, and a deep connection with nature, art, and beauty will help you connect with your spiritual intu-itive sense. Make time for silence and daily contem-plation. Build gratitude into your life daily. Create

a gratitude practice by listing all that you are grateful for in the day that has just passed. Begin to trust the messages, signs, synchronicities, and divinations that occur in your life. They are available to you at all times. Be open to them.

Chapter 9
Power

Power

Opening Invocation

As women, we define power as a network of vital human connections. We are not interested in power for power's sake. Collaboration is a powerful way of getting things done. No one sits at the top, holding rank and status over another.

Opening Ideas for Contemplation

> *Power is good for one thing only: to increase our happiness and the happiness of others. Being peaceful and happy is the most important thing in our lives...*
> — *Thich Nhat Hanh*

> *Many women have more power than they recognize, and they are very hesitant to use it, for they fear they won't be loved."*
> — *Patricia Schroeder*

Introduction to Power

Power is often interpreted as a means to gain dominance over another. It is time to reevaluate this belief system and begin to create power with, not over, another.

In ancestral times, women understood power as connection. They understood how much more they could accomplish and contribute when they used power in a way that benefited the whole. What would the world look like today if we all asked ourselves, "Is there something in me not fully expressed that might contribute to the whole?"

In today's world, the desire for excessive, extreme power has been the engine that drives inequality. In order to bring equality to our lives, we need to address four specific areas that every human being has the right of equal access to: food, healthcare, water, and energy. As I mentioned earlier in this book, we now must eliminate the excessive greed that is played out in violent conflicts across the globe. When power is used to create with, as opposed to hold strength and control over, it becomes meaningful and valuable. When the feminine attributes described in this book are fully lived and integrated into ourselves and our world, we will experience new power and strength, which will benefit all—and claim ownership and create a hierarchy over none.

Women have learned how to relate powerfully in leadership roles by modeling their fathers and their fathers' fathers. In most leadership circles, the feminine attributes are absent; therefore, many women lack an understanding of how to incorporate those attributes into leadership and power at work and in their lives. Many women have adapted to the masculine style of power, for it has allowed them to succeed and fit in.

True feminine power comes from a deep passion within us that informs everything we do. Real leadership has as its source a passion that blends masculine and feminine energy and allows a woman to speak with her own true voice, because she is grounded in a strong sense of her own personal value. In order for this blended passion to come alive in our world, the different ways in which the masculine and feminine wield and hold power will need to be understood and accepted. The world will have to respect both—and it surely needs both. Once the attributes and traits of women are strongly acknowledged and respected, it will no longer be necessary "merely" to take on the traits of men.

When the feminine principles of power and leadership become enlivened in the worlds of business and politics, and also in life, in general, our culture will be more balanced than it is at the moment. Since we have depended for so long on a patriarchal, autocratic style of leadership to run our businesses and rule our culture, it is important for the feminine voice to come forth authentically, so that we can gain a new sense of value and then collaborate in an equal fashion with the masculine. When both voices and styles are at the table, the world will thrive and experience increased integration.

If any one segment of our world is out of balance in the area of power, however, the whole world is out of balance. This is the premise behind integrating power. Hierarchal models of power are no longer appropriate in today's world. Since the feminine sees power as a network of vital human connections, it is clear that power will become more equalized when these vital connections come alive and are fully participating, fully involved, and fully respected. This equalization will lead to peace and harmony.

Inspiring Questions

1. How can you gain a better understanding of your feminine power and begin to use it more fully in the world?

2. How can you lead from your greatest attributes, strengths, and personal power?

3. What support do you now need to step into your power fully?

Witnessing

Make a commitment to deepen your connection to your personal power. Notice where you are comfortable and uncomfortable with power. Make a commitment to express your power more fully in one area of your life. If possible, be witnessed by a friend or someone who supports you.

Power from Contribution and Connection

About power from contribution and connection

As noted, women are not interested in power for power's sake. We tend to evaluate power and judge its relevance and meaning by the contribution it makes to issues in our lives, as well as the substance we bring to the world from expressing power. In order for us to value power in this way, we must have the intention of bringing power to the world from our central core. We need to know who we are and how we fit with others in our lives and our world. When power is used to advance what is right, it brings great delight and supports the web of vital human connections.

Why power from contribution and connection is unique to the feminine

As we know, the feminine values relationships and collaboration. She holds an innate wisdom that teaches that misused power leads to resistance and separation. The feminine experiences life as an interconnected web and looks to others to be a part of the web, to share in decisions, and to build relationships.

How women can use our power from contribution and connection

Women gain a sense of power through our ability to connect to others around us, particularly in relation to a shared, desired outcome. We value the voices, needs, and desires of others and realize that incorporating these aspects allows us to get a clear and balanced understanding of the whole, whether that concerns a family, village, nation, or universe. Having the wisdom to value building relationships and the voices of many makes it impossible for the feminine, at her core, not to consider the needs and desires of others. She understands that power is useless if it is the power of dominance, but that power is strong and essential if it makes a contribution and leads to connection and strength.

Why power from contribution and connection is needed in the world now

When we build sand castles that reach high into the sky and reflect and serve only our own, our immediate family's and our tribe's needs, we isolate ourselves from our ability to make major changes in the world. Powerful change will occur when we come out of our self-centered selves and use our strengths, gifts, and talents for the betterment of all. Knowledge and ownership of our feminine power is the gateway to awakening and elevating our consciousness.

Remember power from contribution and connection when...

...you feel as though your world is small and you are living in a very small way. Remember that you have the natural ability to hold the whole in your vision—because of your increased brain connectivity and your ability inherited from your ancestral sisters to watch the whole village at any given moment. Remember the environment and all of the other areas where life is calling for our attention.

Enlivening power from contribution and connection in your life

As we now know, true power is power that serves and addresses the betterment of all. As Robert Greenleaf's work in the area of "Servant Leadership" teaches us, a true leader finds leadership in service. Notice where your power is being used to enhance only yourself and your needs. Observe where your power is being used with others in mind. It is important that we build our self-esteem and develop great strength as we live our lives. But if our strength is developed merely to support the ego, our lives will be empty. If our power is informed by something greater than ourselves and serves others, we will reach an unsurpassable level of fulfillment and bliss.

Leadership in the World

About leadership in the world

We currently live in a world defined by a masculine definition of power and leadership. This definition has guided our world and set the template from which we operate. The feminine style of leadership in business and overall life, as we know, includes collaboration and relationship building at its core. This approach is slowly making its way towards being accepted in life, in general, and in the business world, specifically. But it is not yet fully integrated or taken as seriously as the masculine, strategic, goal-oriented style of leadership.

As we know, the feminine seeks environments of interrelatedness and collaboration. The feminine is interested in the reason why things are done a certain way and how that relates to the whole organization and its individual parts. This shows that the feminine does hold the ability to think strategically but rather values long-term results over short-term winning. We are at a critical time in the history of our world: we must look closely at how we relate to each other in our work environments, as these environments serve as a powerful ground through which we can learn to improve and deepen our relationships and to develop connection and collaboration.

Why leadership in the world is unique to the feminine

Power and leadership expressed via fairness in our work provide women with the opportunity to step forward and create new paradigms and models for how we work, grow, and create together. When the feminine attributes (collaboration, relationship building, mental flexibility, emotional expressivity, and verbal agility, to name a few) become centrally accepted in our work environments, those environments will be more inviting, creative, and productive than they now are.

How women can use our gift of leadership in the world

In order for women to use their gifts of leadership and power in the work environment, we must fully understand the attributes that we are predisposed towards and actively be willing to express them fully in our work environments. This requires strength and courage, as it may well lead to some vulnerable situations. Showing emotions, building meaningful relationships, and prioritizing collaboration, compassion, and inclusion will define a new way of working. In order to create this kind of environment, women will have to look around their existing work environments and find small ways to integrate these powerful attributes into their daily lives.

How women's leadership is needed in the world now

Because we hold great insight into how to build relationships, show compassion, and keep the needs of the whole in mind, our skills, gifts, and talents are needed to provide leadership in the art of doing business in a whole new way. We have learned that hierarchal models of power are no longer appropriate or effective. It is time to take our inspiration from the web-based style of creating power in order to meet the needs of today's world.

Remember leadership in the world when...

...your strength and power are questioned by another. Remember the gifts and talents that you naturally hold. Bring them forth. Also remember that you have all the natural abilities to be a great leader, if you wish, and that leadership has many definitions. Step into your life and fully show up. Choose small ways to stretch yourself that allow you to do something you have never done, stand for something that you were afraid to stand for before, and use your voice in ways that you, yourself, have not yet heard or even imagined.

Enlivening leadership in the world in your life

Leadership and power are enlivened when our lives are in alignment with what we value and most believe

in. Begin by identifying what you value most in your personal and spiritual life, your work and contribution, and your physical being. Allow yourself to create intentions in each of these areas that will move you to the next level of living. We are put here to expand and grow. Learn from your past experiences and carry them forward, for these experiences will inform your new actions. Remember to listen to the still, quiet voice within. It will give you a sense of guidance that is invaluable and will lead you to make the right choices.

The Feminine Expression of Power

About the feminine expression of power

> *The mother bear will tear you to pieces if*
> *you get between her and her offspring. She*
> *doesn't care if she has any power base when*
> *she is done. It doesn't matter who lines up*
> *on her side. You are simply done for if you*
> *threaten her babies. (Fisher 121)*

Feminine power is not often acknowledged in our world. But in truth, the feminine holds the powers of protection, guidance, understanding, wisdom and—when called upon—physical strength. It is now time to acknowledge the many forms of power that the feminine encompasses. One clear example of how we can call forth our physical strength is when a mother bear fights to protect the life of her small cub. This is a true form of maternal protection and power that stems from both her inner and outer power. Other examples of inner and outer feminine power include the mother who rescues a child pinned under a car or the stories of wild, Celtic women warriors who selflessly defended their communities on horseback with only shields to protect them from their ruthless enemies.

The feminine possesses strength in ways we do not fully acknowledge. Her power is manifested in both the physical and non-physical aspects of life. The day of the weak and helpless female has passed. But we still possess much unrecognized, unused power on all levels. It is now time to claim our power fully in all areas of life.

Why the feminine expression of power is unique

Power in our culture has often been defined historically as individual, physical, masculine strength, whereas we have just seen that the definition of feminine power includes both the physical and more. Throughout history less value has been given to the inner power that is based on wisdom than on the outer, physical power that is shown through force. This, in truth, is simply not a valid way to measure, acknowledge, or value power. Our feminine consciousness is a gateway to a soft but very life-transforming power. We have the ability to see where inequalities exist and changes are needed. Our power base is often in our knowledge and our perceptions. Our highly intuitive abilities and capacity for reading faces and identifying emotions, plus our natural ability to prioritize the creation of valuable networks that we view as essential to human connection all place us in a position where we are not interested in power for power's sake.

The world's new definition of power must include the power to build strong networks through collaboration, soothe a crying child, and listen deeply while providing mediation to bridge differences and heal wounds. It is now time to redefine power to include our wisdom and ability to perceive and do for others what needs to be done, no matter whether physical strength is involved, and to use our natural gifts and talents to make meaningful, essential contributions.

How women can use our gift of the feminine expression of power

When we begin to alter how we define power so that we include both the physical and non-physical sides of power and value both equally, we will also begin to see a shift in our world. The change must first begin within us as we start to value and claim the power that we naturally hold. Our new definition of power will now eliminate power over and update our thinking to encompass power with. When we act in relationship to something or someone and work towards building a common goal, interest, or intention, the outcome runs a far better chance of benefiting many more than would otherwise benefit.

Why the feminine expression of power is needed in the world now

If we look around the world today we see a small percentage of haves and a large percentage of have-nots. Through dominance and determination, our cultures have driven us to a place of inequality, where the voices and needs of most are not taken into consideration. It is the responsibility of the feminine to use her astute gifts of leadership by stepping forward to

create equality in the areas of food, healthcare, the environment and the sharing of information that leads to power. The traits that the feminine is naturally predisposed to hold will build relationships, include everyone, and allow for the needs of all to be involved in directing which way the world will move.

Remember the feminine expression of power when...

...you feel like building something on your own, flying solo, or not including others in your ventures. And when you feel like the solo leader, remember that everyone is a leader, for we all hold power and knowledge that can contribute to a desired outcome. Gain power with and not over. Remember that power is being redefined and that you can redefine it. Create your own definition of power and live your life from this extraordinary place.

Enlivening the feminine expression of power in your life

Enjoy the way that you communicate and share power, and acknowledge that the web you build connects you to others as an evolved form of relating. Continue to build flexible networks that provide greater strength than we possess on our own. And realize that you are a natural relationship-builder and that through the relationships you build, you will both share and gain power.

Achievement and Accomplishment

About achievement and accomplishment

As humans, we are born to have certain desires that actually support our growth. Achievement and accomplishment are essential to us, for they support us in achieving the outcomes we want and fulfilling those human desires. In other words, attempting to achieve our desired outcomes keeps us on track and motivated in life. Indeed, it is healthy to have achievement and accomplishment as rewards in our life. Both provide us with a way of measuring our progress towards—and then experiencing—the desired intentions and outcomes that we dream of. It is crucial that we learn to include collaboration in accomplishing our achievements, for then we involve others who can share in our successes while they create their own wins.

Why achievement and accomplishment are unique to the feminine

The feminine sees accomplishment as sitting at the center of a web of relationships as opposed to the top of a hierarchy. When she, too, sits in this central place, she can respond to needs, take care of the whole, and sustain connection. She knows that when she relates to others in the web in this way, she will develop valuable relationships that will enhance or contribute to everyone's mission and desires as well as her own. She holds unique wisdom in this area.

How women can use our gifts of achievement and accomplishment

Through being aware of the needs of the whole, women create powerful connections that result in engagement and ownership. When we model this style of leadership or interaction, we present a whole new way of relating. Achievement and accomplishment then become an outcome of collaboration. When we live our lives modeling these qualities, we elevate others' thinking, achieve our desired outcomes, and promulgate our way of being in the world.

Why women's achievement and accomplishment are needed in the world now

We need to redefine achievement and accomplishment in order to live in a far more inclusive way than we have come to know to date. When we begin to include and value connection, empathy, and web-like interaction on our own personal path to achieving and accomplishing, we will encourage other women to do the same. There is a famous story that Gail Evans tells in her wonderful book, She Wins, You Win, about a high-achieving woman who climbs the corporate ladder, all the while kicking the women below her as she climbs higher and higher. This is a common experience felt by many women in corporations today. This craziness must stop. We need to replace this behavior with one of mentoring and supporting sisters who follow in our footsteps—trusting that they will respect our knowledge and wisdom and pass it on when it becomes their turn. When we start to set a tone of trust and support, we will create a new culture in all areas of life—a culture that is long overdue among women. Producing outcomes and results can be central to achievement and accomplishment, but no one person needs to stand alone at the top, holding all the power. Again, the idea is to create as many win-win situations as possible and to provide support to as many as we can along the way.

Remember achievement and accomplishment when...

...you find yourself struggling to achieve or accomplish something or feel the need to be at the helm and win a game at the cost of others around you. In those moments, notice that it is possible to include others, listen to their contributions, and come from a more collaborative, expanded place than you currently are.

Enlivening achievement and accomplishment in your life

When we choose to move away from competition—realizing that although competition in the right place can be healthy but that all of life is not just about winning—we remove ourselves from the mad rush to the top. Never hold back from achievement and accomplishment, nor be afraid to stand out, but do not associate your self-worth with these attributes, for you are greater than your achievements and your accomplishments. And when you do move forward in the world to accomplish or achieve, remember why and do it in a way that feels good and enhances your character and overall contribution.

Afterword

Afterword

You have just completed a journey that hopefully will have provided you with greater knowledge about your essential feminine. Life is a wonderful journey full of potential, opportunities, and inspiration. Venture forth with a deeper understanding of the natural feminine attributes and gifts that you hold and are now aware of. As you do the world will be a far better place. Without you and your gifts for the world there would be a void.

Allow life's challenges to provide you with opportunities for more greatness and possibility. For as you embark upon your own personal awakening of your essential feminine you may be questioned and you may be doubted, but most women know they have special unique gifts. Most of us silently nod with each other as we see these gifts enlivened and lived in each other and in the world. It is almost like a secret club. You (we) hold the golden key that will open the door to a whole new, alive and awakened tomorrow. Go forth and enjoy. Live fully and allow your essential feminine to be fully awakened in you and in the world.

Meet you at *www.TheEssentialFeminine.com*.

Bibliography

Bibliography

Brizendine, L. (2006). *The Female Brain*. New York: Morgan Road Books.

Csikszentmihalyi, M. (1996). *Creativity*. New York: Harper Collins.

Fisher, H. (1999). *The First Sex: The Natural Talents of Women and How They Are Changing the World*. New York: Ballantine Publishing Group.

Fletcher, J.K. (1999). *Disappearing Acts*. Cambridge, MA: The MIT Press.

Frenier, C. (1997). *Business and the Feminine Principle: The Untapped Resource*. Burlington, MA: Butterworth-Heinemann.

Gilligan, C. (1982). *In a Different Voice*. Cambridge: Harvard University Press.

Gray, J. (1992). *Men Are from Mars, Women Are from Venus*. New York: Harper Collins.

Helgesen, S. (1990). *The Female Advantage: Women's Ways of Leadership*. New York: Currency Doubleday.

Kipnis, L. (2006). *The Female Thing*. New York: Pantheon.

Maslov, A. (1943). *A Theory of Human Motivation* (originally published in *Psychological Review*, Vol. 50 #4, pp. 370–396)

Palmer, H. (1998). *Inner Knowing*. New York: Tarcher.

Pruetz, J.D. & Bertolani, P. (2007). *Savanna Chimpanzees, Pan Troglodytes Verus, Hunt with Tools*. Current Biology Magazine, 17(5), 412-417.

Schulz, M.L. (2005). *The New Feminine Brain*. New York: Free Press.

Tannen, D. (1990). *You Just Don't Understand: Women and Men Conversation*. New York: William Morrow and Company.

Vaughn, Frances. (1998) *From: Inner Knowing*, Editor, Helen Palmer. New York: Penguin Putnam.

Whitehead, A. N. (1967). *Adventures of Ideas*. paperback, New York: Free Press

Wilson, M.C. (2004). *Closing the Leadership Gap*. New York: Viking Penguin.

About the Author

Maureen Simon

Maureen is founder of The Essential Feminine™ Company (TEF)—a lifestyle and business design company that supports women to create successful powerful lives that incorporates their feminine attributes and gifts. The company provides learning environments and products to support women in claiming, living and leading with their natural strengths and talents. TEF believes that it is now time for women step forward and makes a major contribution in the world. For more information on TEF visit *www.TheEssentialFeminine.com.*

Maureen's experience with women is based on over 25 years of successfully mentoring and guiding women leaders from around the world to create successful lives and businesses that reflect their values. As a social alchemist she addresses women's pertinent issues of social change and transformation. Her work as a pioneering consultant supports women to reduce economic stress, open new channels for their personal and business expression and enhances their ability to access the deeper powers and gifts that each woman holds within their feminine essence. As a highly intuitive business and life designer, Maureen incorporates principles of mysticism, alchemy and social entrepreneurism to achieve focused outcomes and results. Through her work women she supports women to designs lives and business that align with her client's spiritual destiny through an approach that awakens every aspect of the whole woman called, "Awakening The Essential Feminine: Claiming Your Influential Power." Maureen provides individual phone consultations for women worldwide through her private consulting company, Maureen Simon Consulting.

Maureen has worked with women representing a wide range of businesses including *Fortune* 100 corporations, worldwide entertainment and media industries, government, and the creative arts. She mentors both *Fortune* 100 executives as well as leading edge business entrepreneurs. She is founding member of the Global Women's Leadership Network at Santa Clara University's Leavey School of Business in Silicon Valley. Maureen's work has been featured in numerous printed publications, including London's *Vogue, Marie Claire, Self, Women & Home, Good Housekeeping, Bay Area Business Women, Marin Independent Journal, The Financial Times*, and many others. Maureen appears as a regular guest for the London Broadcasting Corporation as well as numerous other radio engagements in both the U.S. and England. She is based in San Francisco, California, and London, England.

The Essential Feminine™
Integrated Life Model

About the Model

The Essential Feminine™ is a philosophy, a way of life and an important component in determining how the human race moves forward. Without Her strong voice, presence and guidance there will remain a vast chasm which will be a great disservice to both the masculine and the feminine and the world we live in.

As we have seen in this book, the feminine lives in many areas of life and holds great depth of understanding care and compassion. Her womb is the source of all life. She is now learning to speak up in all areas of life and to share her vast gifts and awareness. This is her time to live and lead with full knowledge of her gifts.

The model that follows reflects the characteristics of The Essential Feminine™ when she is living fully in all areas of her life. Use the model as a tool to remind yourself of how your natural gifts, attributes and talents can be lived each day of your life.

THE ESSENTIAL FEMININE™
A fully integrated life includes these dynamic qualities...

RHYTHM
Understanding our natural rhythm and capabilities and planning our life accordingly.

ACHIEVEMENT
Fully understanding and fully living to our greatest potential.

SELF RESPECT
Creating time to recharge and rejuvenate and gain a clear perspective in all areas of life (health, business, etc.).

SELF CONFIDENCE
Gaining confidence and strength as we clearly express our voice and trust our intuition.

INTEGRATION
Developing a full understanding of masculine & feminine attributes and utilizing the greatest strength of each.

INTEGRITY
Working and living with care, compassion and mutual respect.

CONTRIBUTION
Knowing your strengths and talents and placing them more powerfully and effectively in the world.

LEADERSHIP
Leading from conviction and belief to unlock the potential in ourselves and others.

SELF KNOWLEDGE
Knowing your values and beliefs and aligning them in your daily life.

INTERCONNECTEDNESS
Acknowledging and living with interconnectedness in relationships and all areas of life.

*Essential Feminine Resources
to Enhance the Quality of Your Life*

Essential Feminine Resources
to Enhance the Quality of Your Life

Designing Life

Awaken the Giant Within: How to Take Immediate Control of Your Mental, Emotional, Physical & Financial Destiny by Anthony Robbins

Business and Leadership

Leadership and the New Science by Meg Wheatley

Synchronicity: The Inner Path of Leadership by Joseph Jaworski

The Seven Habits of Highly Effective People by Stephen R. Covey

Attracting Perfect Customers: The Power of Strategic Synchronicity by Stacey Hall and Jan Erogniez

Rules for Renegades by Christine Comaford-Lynch

Leadership from the Inside Out by Kevin Cashman

Abundance and Finance

The Seven Laws to Spiritual Success by Deepak Chopra

The Secrets of the Millionaire Mind by T. Harv Ecker

Think and Grow Rich by Napoleon Hill

Put More Cash in Your Pocket! by Loral Langemeier (also see *wealthdiva.com/course*)

Diversity

Putting Our Differences to Work: The Fastest Way to Innovation, Leadership, and High Performance by Debbe Kennedy

Barbershops, Bibles, and BET: Everyday Talk and Black Political Thought by Melissa Victoria Harris-Lacewell

Time Use

Mastering Successful Work by Tarthang Tulku

Body and Health

Before the Change: Taking Charge of Your Perimenopause by Ann Louise Gittleman

Ayurvedic Sciences

Perfect Health: The Complete Mind/Body Guide by Deepak Chopra

A Women's Best Medicine by Nancy Lonsdorf, M.D., Veronica Butler, M.D., and Melanie Brown, Ph.D.

The Path of Practice: A Woman's Book of Healing with Food, Breath, and Sound by Bri. Maya Tiwari

Ayurveda: A Life of Balance by Bri. Maya Tiwari

Beauty

Beauty: The Invisible Embrace by John O'Donohue

Communication

You Just Don't Understand: Women and Men in Conversation by Deborah Tannen

Creativity

The Artist's Way: A Spiritual Path to Higher Creativity by Julia Cameron

Relationships

Venus on Fire, Mars on Ice: Hormonal Balance — The Key To Life, Love and Energy by John Gray

People Making by Virgina Satir

Spirit and Mysticism

The Book of Symbols – The Penguin Dictionary of Symbols

Living with Joy by Sanaya Roman

Spiritual Growth by Sanaya Roman

Ask and It Is Given by Esther and Jerry Hicks

The Power of Myth by Joseph Campbell

Positive Energy by Judith Orloff, MD

Celtic Wisdom

Anam Cara by John O'Donohue

The Celtic Spirit by Caitlin Matthews

The Celtic Book of Days by Caitlin Matthews

The Druid Source Book by John Matthews

Kindling the Celtic Spirit by Mara Freeman

Women (also see the bibliography)

The Feminine face of God by Sherry Ruth Anderson and Patricia Hopkins

The Female Brain by Louann Brizendine

Enlightened Power: How Women are Transforming the Practice of Leadership edited by Linda Coughlin, Ellen Wingard, and Keith Hollihan

The First Sex: The Natural Talents of Women and How They are Changing the World by Helen Fisher

Good Girls Don't by Patti Hawn

Index

mental flexibility in women, 44–45
non-verbal communication, 101–102
physical intuitive sense, 132–133
spiritual intuitive sense, 143–144

Brizendine, Louann
on emotional expressivity, 93
The Female Brain , xxiii
on female thought, 40–41
on mental intuitive sense, 139
mind-reading, 135
non-verbal communication, 101

business world
achievement and accomplishment in, 166
author's experience in, 180–181
comfort with ambiguity, 53
emotional expressivity and, 94
feminine leadership in, 157
resources, 188
verbal agility in, 98
women in, xviii

C

care
in innovation, 79
in relationships, 23–26
child-bearing. *see also* motherhood
beauty and, 116–117
care, compassion, and empathy, 23–24
creativity and, 81–82
feminine expression of power, 161
long-term thinking and, 48

collaboration
achievement and accomplishment through, 165–168
power through, 154–156
in relationships, 8–10

comfort with ambiguity, 52–55

communication. *see also* language
non-verbal, 101–104
in relationships, 19–22
resources, 190

community focus
building through emotional expressivity, 94
in thought, 56–59
using imagination in, 70

compassion

importance of, vii
in leadership, 158
power and, 151
through connection and
cooperation, 90
using imagination to
achieve, 69–70

The Essential Feminine
(TEF)
about, 180–181
assessment, xxiv–xxv
defined, xix–xx
model, 184–185
philosophy, xxii–xxiii

estrogen, 31, 35

Evans, Gail, 166

expressing emotion. see
emotional expressivity

F

facial expressions
mental intuitive sense,
139
non-verbal
communication, 102–103

fairness. see equality

feelings. see emotions

The Female Brain
(Brizendine), 41–42, xxiii

feminine attributes
achievement and
accomplishment, 165

appreciation of beauty
and aesthetics, 116–117
care, compassion, and
empathy, 24
collaboration, 8
comfort with ambiguity,
52–53
community focus, 56
connection and
cooperation, 89
creativity and innovation,
81–82
decision-making, 60–61
emotional expressivity,
93–94
emotional intuitive sense,
135–136
expression of power,
161–164
harmony and
peacemaking, 34–35
imagination and vision,
72–73
inclusiveness as, 11–12
interconnectedness,
15–16
leadership, 158
long-term thinking,
48–49
mental intuitive sense,
139–140
non-verbal
communication, 101–102
overview of, xviii–xx

physical intuitive sense,
132–133
power from contribution
and connection, 154
spiritual intuitive sense,
143–144
valuing communication,
19–20
verbal agility, 97

feminine gifts. *see* using
gifts

financial resources, 189

*The First Sex: The Natural
Talents of Women and How
They Are Changing the
World* (Fisher), xxiii

Fisher, Helen
emotional expressivity, 93
feminine expression of
power, 161
imagination, 72
influence of, xxiii
on intuition, 132–133
mental flexibility in
women, 45
mental intuitive sense,
139
non-verbal
communication, 101
on relationships, 4

flexibility, mental, 44–47

focus on community, 56–59

Frenier, C., 49, 141

future, 48–51

G

Gallup, Bonnie, xviii

Gandhi, Mahatma, 30

gifts, using. *see* using gifts

Gilligan, Carol, 19, xxiii

goals
achievement, 165–168
through
interconnectedness, 16

Gray, John, 191

Greenleaf, Robert, 156

H

Hanh, Thich Nhat, 150

harmony
beauty and, 118–119
overview, 30–33
power in, 153
through language, 89
women's approach to,
34–37

hearing
perceiving beauty,
117–118
physical intuition, 133

hierarchies
achievement and
accomplishment, 165
aggression within, 35

vs. community focus,
57–58
vs. networks, 151, 159
relationships and, 4–5
vs. webs, 12
holistic view
achievement and
accomplishment, 166
in decision-making, 60
in female vision, 73
as feminine value, 5
in innovation, 81
interconnectedness and,
16
in intuition, 129
mental flexibility and,
45–46
mental intuitive sense,
142
of relationships, 11
spiritual intuitive sense,
143

I

ideas for contemplation
beauty and aesthetics,
111
creativity and innovation,
78
harmony and
peacemaking, 30
imagination and vision,
68
intuition, 128
language, 86

power, 150
purpose of, xxv
relationships, 4
thought, 40–41
imagination
from female perspective,
72–74
overview, 68–71
In a Different Voice
(Gilligan), xxiii
inclusiveness
community focus, 56–59
in leadership, 158
in relationships, 11–14
individualism
vs. collaboration, 9
vs. interconnectedness, 17
Inner Knowing (Vaughn),
129–130, xxiii
innovation, 78–83
inspiring questions
beauty and aesthetics,
114
creativity and innovation,
80
harmony and
peacemaking, 33
imagination and vision,
71
intuition, 131
language, 88
power, 153
purpose of, xxv
relationships, 6

thought, 43

integration, 185

integrity, 185

interconnectedness
community focus, 56–59
in creativity, 81
in relationships, 15–18

intuition
connection and
cooperation, 91
in decision-making, 62
emotional sense, 135–138

imagination and vision, 73
in language, 91
mental sense, 139–142
overview, 128–131
physical sense, 132–134
power through, 162
spiritual sense, 143–146

invocations
beauty and aesthetics,
110–111
creativity and innovation,
78
harmony and
peacemaking, 30

imagination and vision, 68

intuition, 128
language, 86
power, 150
relationships, 4
thought, 40

K

Kipling, Rudyard, 128

L

language
connection and
cooperation through,
89–92
emotional expressivity in,
93–96
non-verbal
communication, 101–104
overview, 86–88
use in peacemaking, 31
verbal agility, 97–100

leadership
comfort with ambiguity
and, 53–54
in essential feminine, 185
female power and,
157–160
with imagination and
vision, 73
inclusiveness in, 12
power and, 151–152
resources, 188

life, enlivening attributes
in. *see* enlivening in life

life design resources, 188

linear thinking
vs. comfort with
ambiguity, 53

inclusiveness in, 13
leadership in the world,
157–160
overview, 150–153
through communication,
19
through contribution and
connection, 154–156
through harmony and
peacemaking, 31–32,
35–36

problem-solving
comfort with ambiguity,
54
male and female
differences in, 41–42

progress, 165–168

protection
feminine power, 161
with long-term thinking,
49

psychology. *see* thought

Q

questions. *see* inspiring
questions

R

rational thought, 130, 135
receiving, 58
relationships

achievement and
accomplishment through,
165
care, compassion, and
empathy, 23–26
collaboration, 8–10
community focus, 56–59
harmony and
peacemaking in, 37
inclusiveness, 11–14
interconnectedness,
15–18
introduction, 4–7
leadership through, 157
mental flexibility and, 46
resources, 191
valuing communication,
19–22

repression of emotion in
men, 135

research, xviii

resources to enhance life,
188–192

rhythm, 185

S

Schroeder, Patricia, 150
self confidence, 185
self knowledge, 185
self respect, 185
senses
beauty and, 117–118
intuition, 132–134

in language, 97–100

valuing communication, 19

violence

vs. harmony and
peacemaking, 31–32

using imagination and
vision to reduce, 73–74

vision

from female perspective,
72–74

overview, 68–71

vulnerability, 93–94

W

webs

achievement and
accomplishment in, 165

collaboration, 9

community focus, 56–59

connection and
cooperation, 89–92

in decision-making, 61

inclusiveness, 12

interconnectedness, 15–18

power from contribution
and connection, 154–156

power through, 162

Whitehead, Alfred North,
123

wisdom

of elders, 13–14

feminine expression of
power, 162–163

long-term thinking, 48

spiritual intuitive sense,
143–146

Wise, Stephen S., 68

witnessing

beauty and aesthetics,
114

creativity and innovation,
80

harmony and
peacemaking, 33

imagination and vision,
71

intuition, 131

language, 88

power, 153

purpose of, xxvi

relationships, 6–7

thought, 43

women

approach to harmony and
peacemaking, 34–37

author's philosophy,
xxi–xxii

feminine attributes. see
feminine attributes

resources, 191–192

women's groups, xxvii

Staying in Touch

Staying in Touch

Offers and Other Possibilities

The Essential Feminine is a philosophy and
movement that is changing the world as we
know it. It is our intention to support you in
any way that we can, to learn more about your
feminine attributes and gifts so that you may
bring them fully alive in the world. As The
Essential Feminine™ Company continues
to grow, we are increasing our offers and
opportunities worldwide. We encourage you to
stay in touch through the many offers that are
available to you by going to
www.TheEssentialFeminine.com

The Essential Feminine™ Living Room: a one-
time a month Living Room where women worldwide meet to discuss topics of relevance to women
and to network internationally.

The Essential Feminine™ Webinars: internet
and teleconferencing based sessions that provide
information to women on how to create
powerful and successful lives from the
feminine perspective.